《望亭撷粹》编委会

望亭撷粹

运河古镇望亭可移动文物精华

本书编委会 著

苏州大学出版社

图书在版编目（CIP）数据

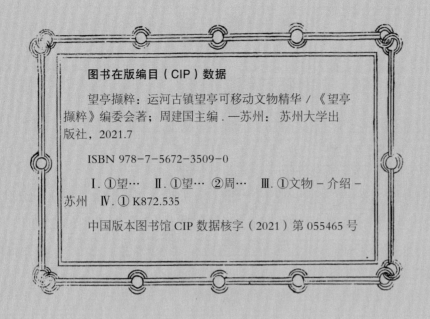

望亭撷粹：运河古镇望亭可移动文物精华 /《望亭撷粹》编委会著；周建国主编 . —苏州：苏州大学出版社，2021.7

ISBN 978-7-5672-3509-0

Ⅰ. ①望… Ⅱ. ①望… ②周… Ⅲ. ①文物 – 介绍 – 苏州 Ⅳ. ① K872.535

中国版本图书馆 CIP 数据核字（2021）第 055465 号

Wangting Xiecui: Yunhe Guzhen Wangting Keyidong Wenwu Jinghua

望亭撷粹：运河古镇望亭可移动文物精华

著　　者　本书编委会
责任编辑　倪浩文
书名书法　郑板桥
出版发行　苏州大学出版社
　　　　　（苏州市十梓街 1 号，215006）
印　　刷　苏州市深广印刷有限公司
开　　本　787 mm×1 092mm　1/8
印　　张　18
字　　数　165 千
版　　次　2021 年 7 月第 1 版
印　　次　2021 年 7 月第 1 次印刷
书　　号　ISBN 978-7-5672-3509-0
定　　价　300.00 元

序 言

Preface

望亭，古名御亭，曾名鹤溪，地处苏州市西北隅，西濒太湖，北隔望虞河与无锡相望，京杭运河过其东境，是一个因水而兴、因河而盛的江南古镇。

望亭的人文历史可以追溯到距今约6000年的新石器时代，此时已有人类在此繁衍生息。夏时属防风氏地区。商末属勾吴国。春秋时期，吴王阖闾曾建长洲苑于境内。秦设吴县后，望亭先后属吴县、泰德县、长洲县等。东汉末年，吴先主孙坚在乌角溪（现沙墩港）和鹤溪（大运河望亭段）交汇处建御亭，形成集镇。隋开皇九年(589)建御亭驿，大业十年（614）置堰闸，并派兵驻守。唐代改御亭为望亭，镇以亭名，并一直沿用至今。

望亭历来为兵家必争之地，历史上集镇数次因战争而毁，几度沿大运河南迁。虽然地表历史风貌变化甚大，但仍有月城、沙墩港、御亭、螺蛳墩、望亭堰等古遗址有迹可寻。近年在诸多古遗址范围内采集到众多石器、陶器、瓷器、铜器和铁器等文物标本，其可辨时代上至新石器时代，下至晚清及民国时期。此外，2015年4月至10月对螺蛳墩遗址进行了抢救性考古发掘工作，发现了一批汉代至清代的古墓葬和1个灰坑，出土了190余件文物标本，不但进一步充实了地方馆藏文物类型，而且为我们了解望亭古代人民的丧葬习俗等提供了翔实资料。

从古至今，望亭一直地处江南水陆交通要道，是南北经济文化的交流重要节点之一。历史上，在隋唐大运河开通之后，大运河逐渐成为望亭的经济大动脉，不但进一步促进了望亭的快速发展，而且也使望亭完成了从传统的“水乡古镇"向新型的“运河古镇”转变。

近年来，在经济迅速发展的同时，望亭镇党委、政府高度重视历史文化底蕴的发掘和文化遗产保护等工作。2019 年 2 月中共中央办公厅、国务院办公厅印发《大运河文化保护传承利用规划纲要》之后，在望亭镇党委、政府的统一布局之下，作为大运河文化带苏州段重要组成部分的千年运河古镇望亭，不但全面恢复了御亭、皇亭碑、驿站等旧址，还系统打造了集遗产保护、文化研究和生态旅游于一体的运河公园暨历史文化街区和大运河百诗碑廊等，还有在建的望亭镇大运河文体馆，都充分传承了历史文化，释放了文化资源活力，解放了文化生产力，展现了望亭人民的时代担当。

为进一步深入学习贯彻习近平总书记对大运河文化带建设的重要批示精神和探索望亭的大运河文化精神内涵，由望亭镇党委、政府组织编写了《望亭撷粹：运河古镇望亭可移动文物精华》一书。为确保入选文物的质量，本书聘请了程义、黄景新等多位有着丰富经验的专家选取本地古遗址采集和考古发掘出土的各类文物标本 140 余件为实体，以历史时间为脉络，在继承以往学者研究的基础上向广大人民群众展现古望亭的人文历史和文化底蕴。

回顾历史是为了更好地展望未来，未来的望亭必将成为大运河文化带上耀眼的文化魅力小镇和生态宜居小镇。望亭也将抓住大运河文化带建设的时代机遇，充分利用和展示本地特色历史文化资源，为经济社会发展贡献新动能，为广大人民群众带来更多的幸福感和获得感。

2021.7

Preface

Zhou Jianguo

Wangting, formerly known as Yuting and Hexi in ancient times, is located in the northwest corner of Suzhou City, bordered by Taihu Lake in the west, and faces Wuxi across the Wangyu River in the north. The Grand Canal crosses its east border. Wangting is an ancient town in the south of the Yangtze River that flourishes because of the water.

The humanistic history of Wangting can be traced back to the Neolithic Age about 6,000 years ago, when humans were already living here. It belonged to Fangfengshi area in the Xia Dynasty. At the end of the Shang Dynasty, it belonged to Gouwu State. During the Spring and Autumn Period, Helu the king of Wu State, once built Changzhou Garden in the territory. After Wu County was established in the Qin Dynasty, Wangting belonged to Wu County, Taide County and Changzhou County successively. At the end of the Eastern Han Dynasty, the ancestor of Wu, Sun Jian, built a royal pavilion at the intersection of Wujiao Creek (now Shadun Port) and Hexi (Wangting Section of the Grand Canal), forming a market town.In the 9th year of Emperor Kaihuang of the Sui Dynasty (589), the Yuting Post was built, and the weir gate was installed in the tenth year of the Great Cause (614), and troops were stationed.In the Tang Dynasty, the Imperial Pavilion was changed to Wang Pavilion, and the town was named after the pavilion, and the name has been used today.

Wangting has always been a battleground for military strategists. Historically, the market town was destroyed by wars and moved south along the Grand Canal several times. Although the historical landscape of the surface has changed greatly, there are still traces of ancient ruins such as Yuecheng, Shadun Port, Yuting, Luojiadun, and Wangtingyan. In recent years, many stone implements, pottery, porcelain, bronzes, and iron artifacts have been collected from many ancient sites, and they can be distinguished from the Neolithic period to the late Qing Dynasty and the Republic of China. In addition, rescue archaeological excavations were carried out on the Luojiudun site from April to October, 2015, and a number of ancient tombs from the Han Dynasty to the Qing Dynasty were discovered, and more than 190 specimens of cultural relics were unearthed, which not only further enriches the types of cultural relics in the local collection, but also provides us with detailed information on the funeral customs of the ancient people in Wangting.

From ancient times to the present, Wangting has always been located on the water and land transportation in the south of the Yangtze River, and is one of the important nodes of economic and cultural exchanges between the North and the South.Historically, after the opening of the Grand Canal in the Sui and Tang Dynasties, the Grand Canal gradually became the economic artery of Wangting, which not only further promoted the rapid development of Wangting, but also enabled Wangting to complete the transition from the traditional "water town" to the new "canal ancient town".

In recent years, with the rapid economic development, Wangting Town Party committee and People's Government has attached great importance to the discovery of historical and cultural heritage and the protection of cultural heritage. After the General Office of the Central Committee of the Communist Party of China and the General Office of the State Council issued the "Plan for the Protection, Inheritance and Utilization of the Grand Canal Culture" in February 2019, under the unified layout of the People's Government of Wangting Town, as an important part of the Suzhou section of the Grand Canal Cultural Belt, Wangting, the ancient town of the Millennium Canal, has not only fully restored the old sites such as Yuting, Huangting Monument and the Post Station, but also systematically created a canal park integrating heritage protection, cultural research and eco-tourism.

It is also a historical and cultural block, as well as the Wangting Town Grand Canal Cultural and Sports Center and the Grand Canal Hundred Poems Stele Gallery, etc. All of them have fully inherited history and culture, released the vitality of cultural resources, liberated cultural productivity, and demonstrated the role of the people in Wangting.

In order to further study and implement the important instructions of General Secretary Xi Jinping on the construction of the Grand Canal Cultural Belt and to explore the spiritual connotation of the Grand Canal culture of Wangting, Wangting Town organized and compiled the book named *Excerpts of Wangting: The Essence of the Movable Cultural Relics of Ancient Canal Town Wangting*. In order to ensure the quality of the selected cultural relics, we hired many experienced experts such as Cheng Yi, Huang Jingxin to select more than 140 specimens of various cultural relics unearthed from local ancient site collections and archaeological excavations as entities, taking historical time as the context, and presenting the humanities, history and cultural heritage of ancient Wangting to the masses based on previous scholars' research.

Looking back on history is to better look forward to the future. In the future, Wangting will surely become a dazzling cultural charm town and ecologically livable town on the Grand Canal Cultural Belt. Wangting will also seize the opportunities of the times in the construction of the Grand Canal Cultural Belt, make full use of and display local characteristics of historical and cultural resources, contribute new momentum to economic and social development, and bring more happiness and sense of gain to the general public.

螺蛳墩遗址考古发掘与收获

苏州市考古研究所　周官清

螺蛳墩遗址位于江苏省苏州市相城区望亭镇四旺村四组黄泥岗东，东侧紧邻京杭大运河，北侧为月城河，当地俗称“螺蛳墩”。遗址原状为一残存土墩，现存地势南高北低，南、西、北三面环水，东西长约90米，南北宽约60米。

为配合四旺村环境整治工程，2015年4月至10月，苏州市考古研究所对螺蛳墩进行了抢救性考古发掘工作，发掘总面积760多平方米，发现17处遗迹现象，其中墓葬16座、灰坑1个，出土各类遗物190余件。

螺蛳墩原始地貌

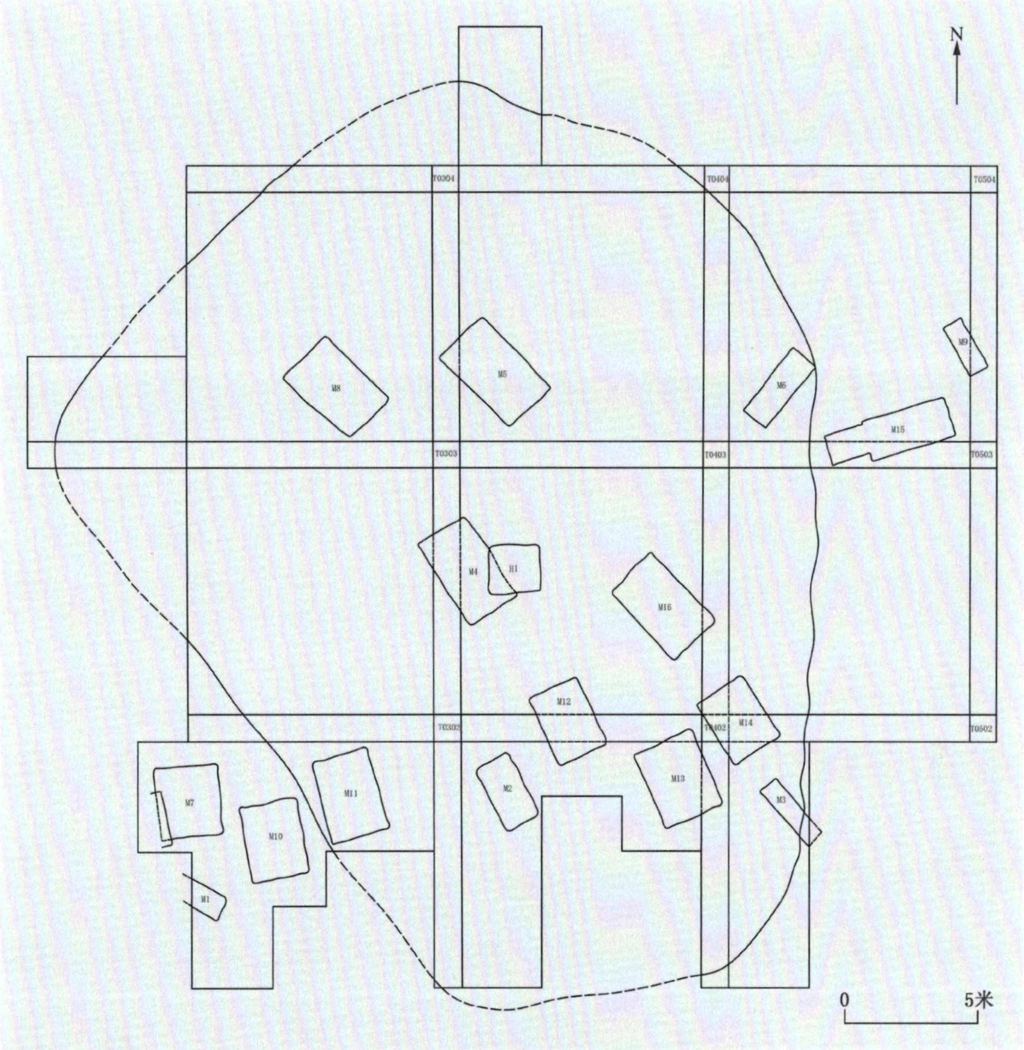

螺蛳墩遗址考古发掘总平面图

M8 清理发掘工作照

一、遗迹举例

1. 竖穴土坑墓

本次考古发现竖穴土坑墓 9 座，形制大小略有不同，其中 M1、M3 和 M6 相似，为瘦长方形，M15 为刀形，M2、M4、M5、M8 和 M16 相似，为宽长方形，该类墓葬在形制上呈现了一定的时代差异性。

M3 位于发掘区东南部，局部延伸进入东壁内，方向 135°。平面呈长方形，竖穴土坑墓，长 2.7 米、宽 0.66 米、深 0.66 米。墓室内填黄褐色土，夹杂少许黑土块。墓室内未发现葬具。墓室西北部发现有少许墓主肢骨，腐朽严重。墓室中部多处发现有铜钱，但腐朽粉化严重，难以提取，可辨钱文均为“开元通宝”，墓室

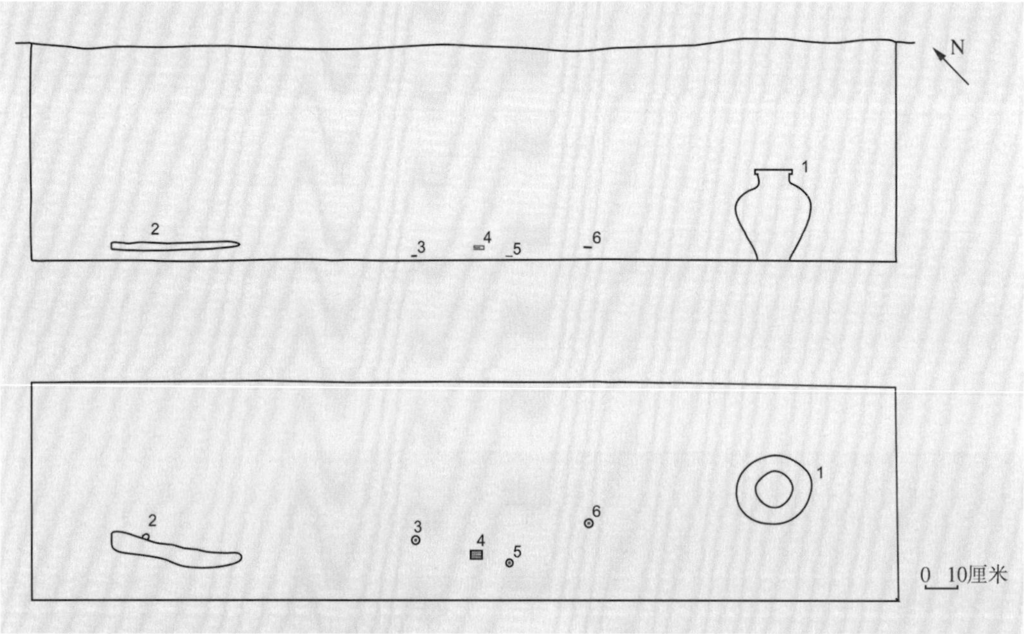

M3 平剖视图

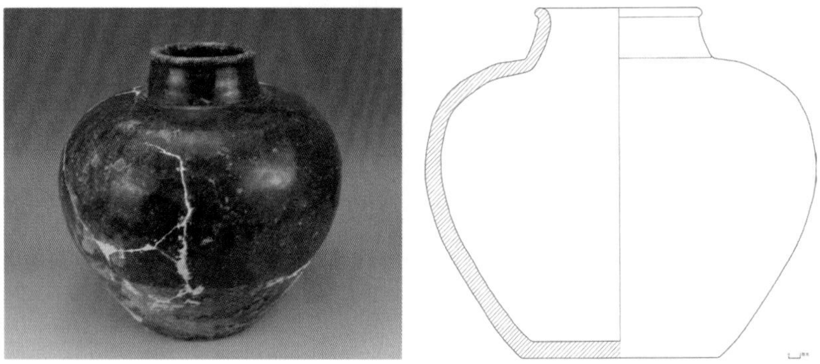

M3 出土陶壶

南端发现1件釉陶壶。

M6位于发掘区东北部，方向213°。平面呈长方形，竖穴土坑墓，长2.8米、宽1米、深0.35米。墓室内填充黄褐色土，质地较松软。墓室中部残存有长方形棺痕和少许棺钉。在棺痕内发现墓主骨架，但腐朽严重，墓主头骨位于墓室西端，仰身直肢葬。在墓主头骨的左上方发现1件带柄铜镜。墓室底部有一层红色细沙石铺垫。

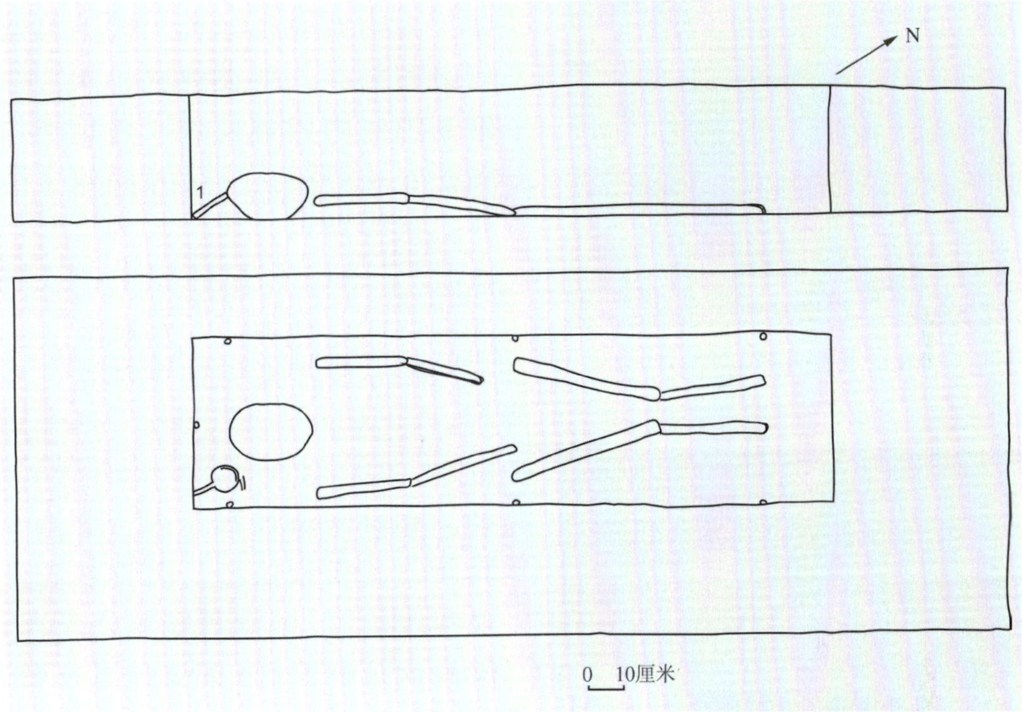

M6 平剖视图

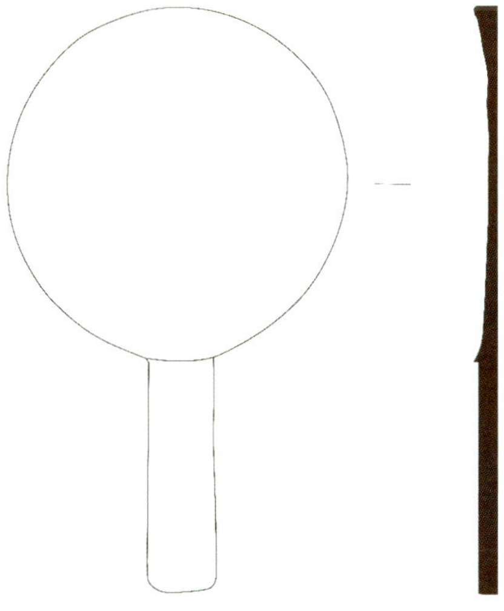

M6 出土铜镜

M15 发掘照

M16 发掘照

M15位于发掘区中东部，方向250°。平面呈“刀”形，竖穴土坑墓，长4.65米、宽1.7米、深0.7米。墓葬由墓道和墓室组成。墓道位于墓室西端偏北，长1.55米、宽1.3米，直壁平底。墓室位于墓道东侧，在墓室中部发现两副棺木残痕，并残存有棺钉，为一墓双棺结构。墓主骨骼均腐朽无存，葬姿葬式不明。在南侧棺痕内西端发现1件铜釜，腐朽碎裂严重，中部发现较多散乱放置的铜钱，可辨均为“开元通宝”；在北侧棺痕内中部发现少量铜钱，亦为“开元通宝”。

M16位于发掘区中部，方向315°。平面呈长方形，竖穴土坑墓，长3.65米、宽2.1米、深1.3米。墓室内填黄褐色土，夹杂白灰块，土质较疏松。墓室底部发现两副棺痕。墓主骨骼腐朽无存，仅残存几枚牙齿，葬姿葬式不明。在西侧棺痕内北端发现1件铜镜和1件小陶罐，中部偏西发现两枚铜钱，在东侧墓室北端发现铜镜、石黛板、铁削刀各1件，中部偏西发现铁刀1件，铜钱3串，中部偏东发现铁剑1把。另在墓室南部棺外发现1件铁鼎、1件铁釜、3件陶壶和2件红陶罐等。

2. 石盖板砖室墓

石盖板砖室墓共计发现6座，

形制结构相近，上部用石盖板封盖，下部为砖砌墓室，其中 M7、M10、M11 和 M12、M13、M14 各为一组，皆呈“品”字形分布，在时代上较为一致，有一定的族属关系。

M10 位于发掘区西南部，方向 171°。平面呈长方形，竖穴土坑石盖板砖室墓，一墓双室，长 2.75 米、宽 2.3 米、墓室深 0.98 米。墓室外壁为竖穴土圹，内壁为青砖纵向平铺垒砌的砖壁，砖壁上部有石条墓框，其上封盖石盖板。两墓室葬具均严重腐朽无存，难以辨别，仅发现少许棺钉。墓主骨骼腐朽粉化严重，仅有零星残余，葬姿葬式不明。西侧墓室中部发现 1 枚铜镜，南端壁龛内发现 1 件青花瓷罐，东侧墓室中部发现 1 枚铜镜，南端发现 1 个硬陶瓶。

3. 砖室券顶墓

砖室券顶墓仅发现 1 座，编号 M9，形制比较窄小。

M9 位于发掘区东北部，方向 145°。平面呈长方形，竖穴土坑砖室券顶墓，长 2.05 米、宽 0.7 米、深 1.2 米。墓室外壁为竖穴土圹，内壁为青砖纵向平铺垒砌的砖壁，砖壁上部为青砖垒砌券顶。

M10 发掘照

M10 出土青花瓷罐

M10 出土铜镜

M9 发掘照

墓室内填充较多黑灰色淤土。墓室底部四角各发现一块垫棺青砖，但棺木腐朽无存。墓主骨骼腐朽粉化严重，依稀可辨头骨和部分肢骨，仰身直肢葬。未发现随葬遗物。

4. 灰坑

本次发现灰坑 1 个，编号 H1，向下打破 M4 东南部。平面呈不规则长方形，开口长 2 米、宽 1.8 米，底长 1.5 米、宽 1.3 米、深 1.3 米。口大底小，斜壁，底较平。其内填土为一次性堆积形成，壁面较为光滑。包含有大量的青砖块、石块、青瓷片、陶片和残瓦片等，遗物堆积凌乱，疑似盗洞。

二、初步认识

螺蛳墩遗址南半部因建造住房及平整货运场已经不复存在，北半部堆积保存良好，但因近代造坟、耕作，对地表扰动严重，根据散落遗物，推测应有多处明清墓葬被扰乱破坏。

从考古发掘墩体剖面堆积情况来看，螺蛳墩墩体由多个历史时期不断加筑堆积形成。螺蛳墩最早的核心堆积为黄褐色土夹杂灰白土块堆积形成，略呈馒头状堆积，范围较小，其上中部坐落多个汉代墓葬。后来墩体在向四周加筑和扩大的过程中逐渐坐落有唐、宋、明等历史时期墓葬。

根据本次发现遗迹的开口层位和出土遗物情况来看，M2、M4、M5、M8和M16为汉代墓葬，M1、M3和M15为唐代墓葬，M6为宋代墓葬，M7、M10、M11、M12、M13和M14为明代墓葬，M9为清代墓葬，H1为明代灰坑。

三、结语

本次发掘出土了陶、铜、铁、琉璃等各质地遗物190余件（组），主要器形有陶罐、陶壶、铜釜、铁鼎、琉璃耳珰、石黛板等，分属汉、唐、宋、明、清等时代，进一步丰富了地方馆藏文物类型，为相关器物研究提供了实物资料。

本次考古发掘证实螺蛳墩遗址是一处始于汉终于清的高台墓地，其上墓葬形制有竖穴土坑墓、石盖板砖室墓和砖室券顶墓等，时代特征明显，同时期墓葬排列规划有序，有一定的家族墓地特征，为研究古代望亭地区丧葬习俗及其演变提供了详实参考资料。

Archaeological Excavation and Rewards at Luosidun Site

Suzhou Institute of Archaeology Zhou Guanqing

The Luosidun site is located in the east of Huangnigang, Group 4, Siwang Village, Wangting Town, Xiangcheng District, Suzhou City, Jiangsu Province. It is adjacent to the Grand Canal to the east and Yuecheng River to the north. Locally known as "Luosidun". The site is a remnant mound in its original state. The existing terrain is high in the south and low in the north. It is surrounded by water on three sides in the south, west and north. It is about 90 meters long from east to west and 60 meters wide from north to south.

In order to cooperate with the environmental improvement project of Siwang Village, from April to October 2015, Suzhou Institute of Archaeology carried out rescue archaeological excavation on the snail pier. The total area of excavation was more than 760 square meters and 17 sites were found, including 16 tombs , 1 ash pit, and more than 190 various relics were unearthed.

Ⅰ. Examples of the sites

1. Vertical Cavern Tomb

This archeological discovery of 9 vertical cave earth pit tombs are slightly different in shape and size. Among them, M1, M3 and M6 are similar and are thin and rectangular. M15 is knife-shaped, and M2, M4, M5, M8 and M16 are similar, and are wide and rectangular. This type of tomb has a certain age difference in shape.

M3 is located in the southeast of the excavation area, partially extending into the east wall, with a direction of 135°. The plane is rectangular, and the tomb is 2.7 meters long, 0.66 meters wide, and 0.66 meters deep. The tomb is filled with yellowish brown soil, mixed with a little black soil. No burial objects were found in the tomb. A few bones of the tomb owner's main limbs were found in the northwest part of the tomb, which was seriously decayed. Copper coins were found in many places in the middle of the tomb, but they were so decayed and pulverized that they were difficult to extract. The recognizable coins were all "Kaiyuan Tongbao". A glazed earthenware pot was found at the southern end of the tomb .

M6 is located in the northeast of the excavation area with a direction of 213°. The plane is rectangular, and the tomb is 2.8 meters long, 1 meter wide and 0.35 meters deep. The tomb is filled with yellow-brown soil, with a soft texture. There are rectangular coffin marks and a few coffin nails remaining in the middle of the tomb. The skeleton of the tomb owner was found in the coffin scars, but it was seriously decayed. The skull of the tomb owner was located at the west end of the tomb and was buried with straight limbs. A bronze mirror with a handle was found at the upper left of the tomb owner's skull. There is a layer of red fine sand and stone paving at the bottom of the tomb.

M15 is located in the middle east of the excavation area, with a direction of 250°. The plane is in the shape of a "knife", with a vertical cavern earth pit 4.65 meters long, 1.7 meters wide and 0.7 meters deep. The tomb consists of a tomb passage and a tomb chamber. The passage, located at the north-west end of the tomb, is 1.55 meters long and 1.3 meters wide, with straight walls and flat bottom. The chamber is located on the east side of the passage. Two coffin remnants and some coffin nails are found in the middle of the chamber. It is a tomb with double coffin structure. Ther are all decayed, and the burial position is unknown. A copper cauldron was found at the west end of the coffin scar on the south side. It was severely decayed and fragmented. In the middle of the chamber, there were many scattered copper coins, all of which could be identified as "Kaiyuan Tongbao"; a small amount of copper coins were found in the middle of the coffin scar on the north side, also known as "Kaiyuan Tongbao".

M16 is located in the middle of the excavation area with a direction of 315°. The plane is rectangular, with a vertical cavern earth pit 3.65 meters long, 2.1 meters wide, and 1.3 meters deep. The tomb is filled with yellowish brown soil, mixed with white ash blocks, and the soil is relatively loose. Two coffin marks were found at the bottom of the tomb. The bones of the tomb owner are decayed, only a few teeth remain, and the burial position is unknown. A bronze mirror and a small clay pot were found at the north end of the coffin on the west side. Two copper coins were found west of the middle. One bronze mirror, a stone slab and an iron knife were found at the north end of the east tomb, and the middle part was west. An iron knife was found west of the middle. Three strings of copper coins, and an iron sword was found east of the middle. In addition, an iron tripod, an iron kettle, three clay pots and two red clay pots were found outside the coffin in the southern part of the tomb.

2. Stone-cover brick chamber tomb

A total of 6 stone-covered brick chamber tombs with similar shapes and structures have been discovered. The upper part is covered with a stone cover, and the lower part is a brick chamber. Among the six tombs, M7, M10, M11 and M12, M13, M14 are in two different set respectively, distributed like the Chinese character "pin". They are relatively consistent in the times and have a certain ethnic relationship.

M10 is located in the southwest of the excavation area, with a direction of 171°. The plan is rectangular, with a vertical cavern earth pit with a stone cover and a brick chamber. It is a tomb with two chambers, 2.75 meters long, 2.3 meters wide, and 0.98 meters deep. The outer wall of the tomb is a vertical cavern, and the inner wall is made of blue bricks and laid vertically. The upper part of the brick wall has a stone tomb frame, which is covered with a stone cover. The burial utensils in the two tombs were severely decayed and unrecognizable. Only a few coffin nails were found. The bones of the tomb owner are severely decayed and powdered, with only scattered remnants, and the burial style is unknown. A bronze mirror was found in the middle of the western tomb. A blue and white porcelain jar was found in the niche at the southern end. A bronze mirror was found in the middle of the eastern tomb, and a hard pottery vase was found at the southern end.

3. Brick room voucher top tomb

Only one tomb in the brick room, numbered M9, is found at the top of the tomb, which is relatively narrow in shape.

M9 is located in the northeast of the excavation area, with a direction of 145°. The plane is rectangular, with a vertical hole earth pit and brick chamber top tomb, which is 2.05 meters long, 0.7 meters wide, and 1.2 meters deep. The outer wall of the cemetery is a vertical cavern, the inner wall is a brick wall made of blue bricks and laid vertically, and the upper part of the brick wall is a roof of blue bricks. The tomb is filled with more dark gray silt. A padded coffin blue brick was found at each of the four corners at the bottom of the tomb, but the coffin was rotten. The bones of the tomb owner were severely decayed and powdered. The skull and part of the limb bones were faintly distinguishable, and he was buried straight on his back. No burial relics were found.

4. Ash pit

One ash pit, numbered H1, was found this time, breaking down to the southeast of M4. The plane is irregularly rectangular, the opening is 2 meters long, 1.8 meters wide, and the bottom is 1.5 meters long, 1.3 meters wide, and 1.3 meters deep. The mouth and the bottom are small, with inclined walls and flat bottom. The filling soil is formed at one time and the wall surface is relatively smooth. Containing a large number of blue bricks, stones, celadon shards, pottery shards and broken tiles, etc., the relics are piled up in a mess and are suspected to be stolen holes.

Ⅱ. Preliminary understanding

The southern half of the Luosidun site no longer exists due to the construction of houses and the leveling of freight yards, and the northern half is well preserved. However, due to the construction of graves and farming in modern times, the ground has been disturbed severely. Judging from the scattering relics, the tombs were disturbed and destroyed.

Judging from the accumulation of the archaeological excavation pier body section, the body part of the snail pier was formed by the continuous accumulation of multiple historical periods. The earliest core accumulation of the snail pier was formed by the accumulation of yellow-brown soil mixed with grayish-white soil blocks, which was slightly stacked like a steamed bun with a small area. There are many Han Dynasty tombs in the upper and middle parts. Later, during the process of adding and expanding the pier, there were tombs of Tang, Song, Ming and other historical periods.

According to the location of the opening and the unearthed relics, M2, M4, M5, M8 and M16 are Han Dynasty tombs, M1, M3 and M15 are Tang Dynasty tombs, M6 are Song Dynasty tombs, and M7, M10, M11, M12, M13 and M14 are Ming Dynasty tombs, M9 is Qing Dynasty tombs, and H1 is Ming Dynasty ash pit.

Ⅲ. Conclusion

More than 190 relics (groups) of various textures such as pottery, copper, iron and colored glaze were unearthed in this excavation. The main vessel shapes are clay pots, pots, copper kettles, iron tripods, colored glaze ears, stone slabs, etc. The Han, Tang, Song, Ming, Qing and other eras further enriched the types of cultural relics in local collections and provided physical data for the research on related artifacts.

The archaeological excavation confirmed that the Luosidun site was a Gaotai cemetery that began in the Han Dynasty and ended in the Qing Dynasty. The tombs on it consist of vertical cave earth pit tombs, stone-covered brick chamber tombs, and brick chamber voucher tombs. The characteristics of the era are obvious. The tombs of the period are arranged in an orderly manner and have certain characteristics of family cemeteries, which provide detailed reference materials for the study of ancient funeral customs and their evolution in Wangting area.

目录

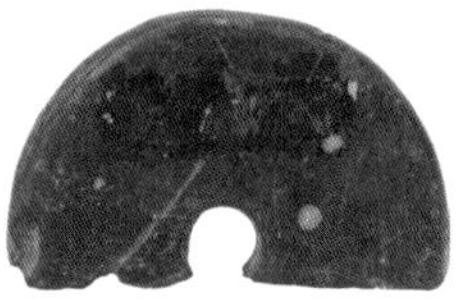

001 石钺
良渚 2

002 石钺
良渚 2

003 石犁
新石器 4

004 石斧
良渚 6

005 石斧
良渚 6

006 石斧
良渚 8

007 石斧
良渚 8

008 石锛
良渚 10

009 石锛
良渚 12

010 石刀
良渚 12

011 石刀
良渚 14

012 石矛
良渚 16

013 石镞
良渚 16

014 石镞
良渚 18

015 石镞
良渚 18

016 石镞
良渚 20

017 石镞
良渚 20

018 陶网坠
良渚 22

019 陶网坠
良渚 24

020 陶网坠
良渚 26

021 陶网坠
良渚 28

022 石纺轮
良渚 30

023 石纺轮
良渚 32

024 陶纺轮
良渚 34

025 陶纺轮
良渚 36

026 玉环
良渚 38

027 玉珠
良渚 40

028 陶杯
良渚 42

029 陶罐
春秋 44

030 陶罐
春秋 46

031 原始瓷盅
春秋 48

032 陶罐
春秋战国 50

033 陶罐
战国 52

034 铜刀
战国 54

035 铜刀
战国 54

036 陶罐
汉 56

037 陶罐
汉 58

038 陶罐
汉 60

039 陶罐
汉 62

040 陶罐
汉 64

041 陶罐
汉 66

042 釉陶罐
汉 68

043 釉陶罐
汉 70

044 釉陶罐
汉 72

045 釉陶瓿
汉 74

046 釉陶瓿
汉 76

047 釉陶瓿
汉 78

048 釉陶瓿
汉 80

049 陶壶
汉 82

050 陶壶
汉 84

051 陶壶
汉 86

052 陶壶
汉 88

053 陶壶
汉 90

054 陶壶
汉 92

055 釉陶壶
汉 94

056 陶壶
汉 96

057 釉陶壶
汉 98

058 釉陶壶
汉 100

059 釉陶壶
汉 102

060 釉陶壶
汉 104

061 釉陶壶
汉 106

062 釉陶壶
汉 108

063 釉陶壶
汉 110

064 釉陶壶
汉 112

065 陶麟趾金
汉 114

066 陶井圈
汉 116

067 陶筒瓦
汉 118

068 陶筒瓦
汉 120

069 陶瓦当
汉 122

070 陶瓦当
汉 124

071 陶瓦当
汉 126

072 石黛板
汉 128

073 石黛板
汉 130

074 铜镜
汉 132

075 铜镜
汉 134

076 铜镜
汉 136

077 铜镜
汉 138

078 铜镜
汉 140

079 铜镜
汉 142

080 铜带钩
汉 144

081 铜带钩
汉 146

082 铜釜
汉 148

083 五铢铜钱
汉 150

084 铁釜
汉 152

085 铁鼎
汉 154

086 琉璃耳珰
汉 156

087 青砖
六朝 158

088 青砖
六朝 160

089 青瓷碗
唐 162

090 釉陶罐
唐 164

091 釉陶罐
唐 166

092 陶碾轮
唐宋 168

093 陶碾轮
唐宋 168

094 陶瓦当
唐 170

095 青釉瓷碗
五代 172

096 青瓷碗
宋 174

097 黑釉盏
宋 176

098 青瓷盂
宋 178

099 黑釉罐
宋 180

100 青釉执壶
宋 182

101 青釉执壶
宋 184

102 陶水注
宋 186

103 韩瓶
宋 188

104 铜镜
宋 190

105 陶鸭形砚
宋 192

106 铜印章
元 194

107 青白釉荷叶盖罐
元 196

108 青瓷香炉
明 198

109 青花瓷罐
明 200

110 青花瓷碗
明 202

111 青花瓷盘
明 204

112 青瓷盏
明 206

113 釉陶罐
明 208

114 韩瓶
明 210

115 铜镜
明 212

116 铜镜
明 214

117 铜镜
明 216

118 铜镜
明 218

119 铜镜
明 220

120 铜镜
明 220

121 银耳勺
明 222

122 故吴孺人杨氏墓志铭
明 224

123 明故秋淮处士居君伯高墓志铭
明 226

124 青花瓷杯
清 228

125 青花瓷碗
清 230

126 青花瓷盘
清 232

127 青花瓷碾钵
清 234

128 青花瓷洗
清 236

129 青花瓷笔洗
清 238

130 青花瓷笔筒
清 240

131 青花瓷茶叶罐
清 242

132 青花瓷将军罐
清 244

133 青花印泥盒
清 246

134 黄釉瓷盘
清 248

135 铜碗
清 250

136 石权
明清 252

137 石权
明清 252

138 蠲免银税碑
清 254

139 木印章
清末民初 256

140 浅绛彩山水棒槌瓶
民国 258

141 青花瓷碗
民国 260

望亭镇地志馆

001　石钺
Stone Axe

良渚
月城遗址采集
长 15.4 厘米、刃宽 11.5 厘米、厚 0.8 厘米

青石质。器身近似长方形，扁平，背部略窄，刃部略宽。平背，双面弧刃，器身上部有一圆形对钻孔。器身中部略厚，四边略薄，通体磨光。

002　石钺
Stone Axe

良渚
月城遗址采集
长 9.2 厘米、刃宽 8 厘米、厚 1.3 厘米

青石质。器身呈梯形，扁平。平背，双面弧刃，中上部有上下两个圆形对钻孔，上孔残缺一半。器身中部略厚，四边略薄，通体磨光。

003　石犁
Stone Plow

新石器
月城遗址采集
宽 28.3 厘米、高 27.3 厘米、厚 1.8 厘米

整体呈三角形，器身扁平，上端有一凸形柄，中部有一圆形对凿孔，单面开刃。刃部磨光，其余部分较粗糙。石质坚硬，呈青灰色。

004　石斧
Stone Axe

良渚
月城遗址采集
长 15.4 厘米、刃宽 11.5 厘米、厚 0.8 厘米

青石质。器身似倒“T”形，扁平。斧身近似半月形，斧背中部有凸柄，双面弧刃，扁薄。器身较厚重，制作略粗糙。

005　石斧
Stone Axe

良渚
月城遗址采集
长 12.2 厘米、刃宽 13 厘米、厚 1.7 厘米

青石质。器身似梯形，扁平。斧背略窄，斧刃略宽，双面弧刃，扁薄。器身较厚重，制作较粗糙。

006　石斧
Stone Axe

良渚
月城遗址采集
长 11.2 厘米、刃宽 14.6 厘米、柄宽 5.7 厘米、厚 2 厘米

青石质。器身似靴形。斧背较宽厚，背上一端有凸柄，斧刃较宽，双面弧刃，扁薄。器身制作较粗糙。

007　石斧
Stone Axe

良渚
月城遗址采集
长 16.8 厘米、刃宽 15.4 厘米、柄宽 6.6 厘米、厚 2.5 厘米

青石质。器身似倒“T”形，扁平。斧背较宽厚，背上中部凸柄，斧刃较宽，双面弧刃，扁薄。器身制作较粗糙。

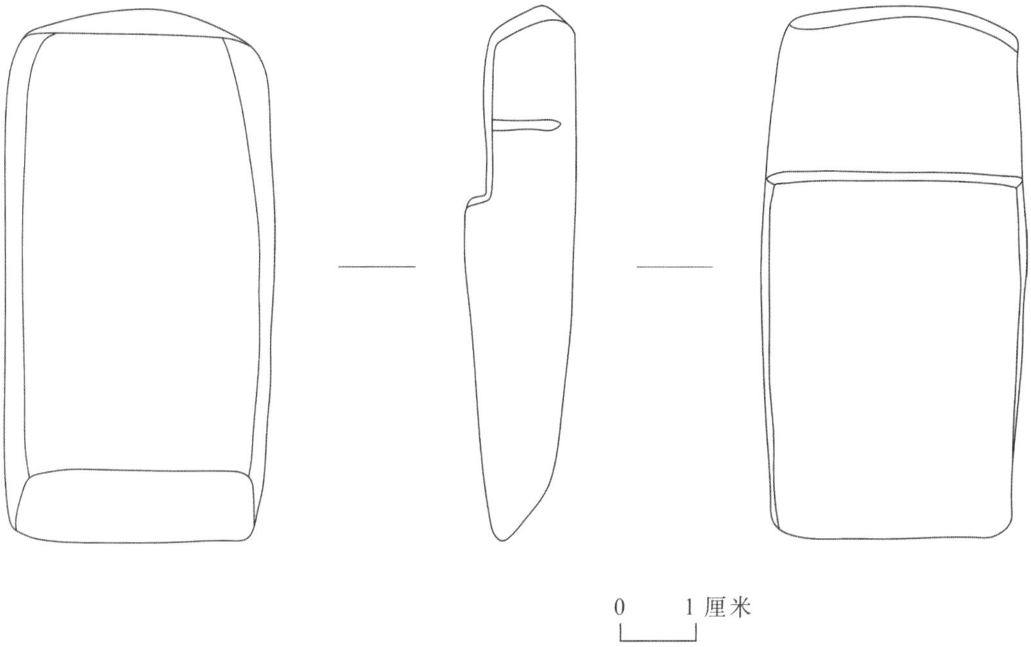

008　石锛
Stone Adzes

良渚
月城遗址采集
长 6.8 厘米、宽 3.5 厘米、厚 1.3 厘米

青石质。器身呈长方体形，扁平。器身中上部一面有段，一面无段，无段一面单面开刃。通体磨光。

009　石锛
Stone Adzes

良渚
月城遗址采集
长 23.5 厘米、宽 10.6 厘米、厚 1.8 厘米

青石质。器身呈长方体形，窄长扁平。一端有单面斜刃，局部残缺。通体磨光。

010　石刀
Stone Knife

良渚
月城遗址采集
长 26.8 厘米、宽 11 厘米、厚 2.5 厘米

青石质。器身似半月形，扁平。弧背，背部较厚重，圆弧形双面刃，刃部扁薄，刀尖残缺，刀柄宽厚。器身制作较粗糙。

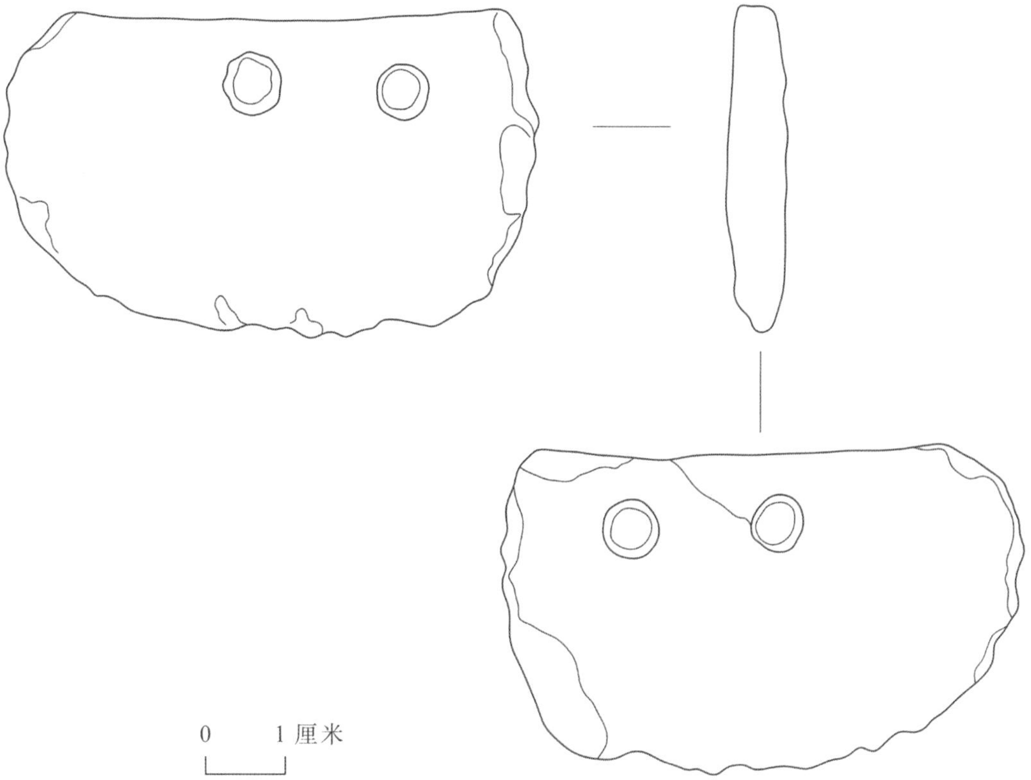

011 石刀
Stone Knife

良渚
月城遗址采集
长 6.8 厘米、宽 4 厘米、厚 0.7 厘米

青石质。器身近似半圆形，扁平。刀背较平直，弧形双面刃，刃部残损严重，近背部有两个圆形对钻孔。器身制作较粗糙。

012　石矛
Stone Spear

良渚

月城遗址采集

长 13.7 厘米、宽 4.4 厘米、厚 1.8 厘米

青石质。器身似梭形，瘦长，中部宽厚，边缘扁薄。器身两侧开双面刃，矛尖尖圆，圆柄粗短，柄上有穿孔。器身制作较粗糙。

013　石镞
Stone Arrowhead

良渚

月城遗址采集

长 4.3 厘米、宽 1.8 厘米、厚 0.8 厘米

青石质。器身宽短，三棱形镞头，圆柱形镞尾。通体磨光。

014　石镞
Stone Arrowhead

良渚
月城遗址采集
长 6.2 厘米、宽 1.4 厘米、厚 0.7 厘米

青石质。器身呈柳叶形，瘦长，三棱形镞头。通体磨光。

015　石镞
Stone Arrowhead

良渚
月城遗址采集
长 12 厘米、宽 2.2 厘米、厚 1.2 厘米

青石质。器身呈柳叶形，瘦长，三棱形镞头，圆柱形镞尾。通体磨光。

016　石镞
Stone Arrowhead

良渚
月城遗址采集
长 8 厘米、宽 2.3 厘米、厚 1 厘米

青石质。器身呈柳叶形，瘦长，三棱形镞头，镞尾残缺。通体磨光。

017　石镞
Stone Arrowhead

良渚
月城遗址采集
长 9.5 厘米、宽 1.1 厘米、厚 0.6 厘米

青石质。器身呈细柳叶形，瘦长，三棱形镞头，圆柱形镞尾。通体磨光。

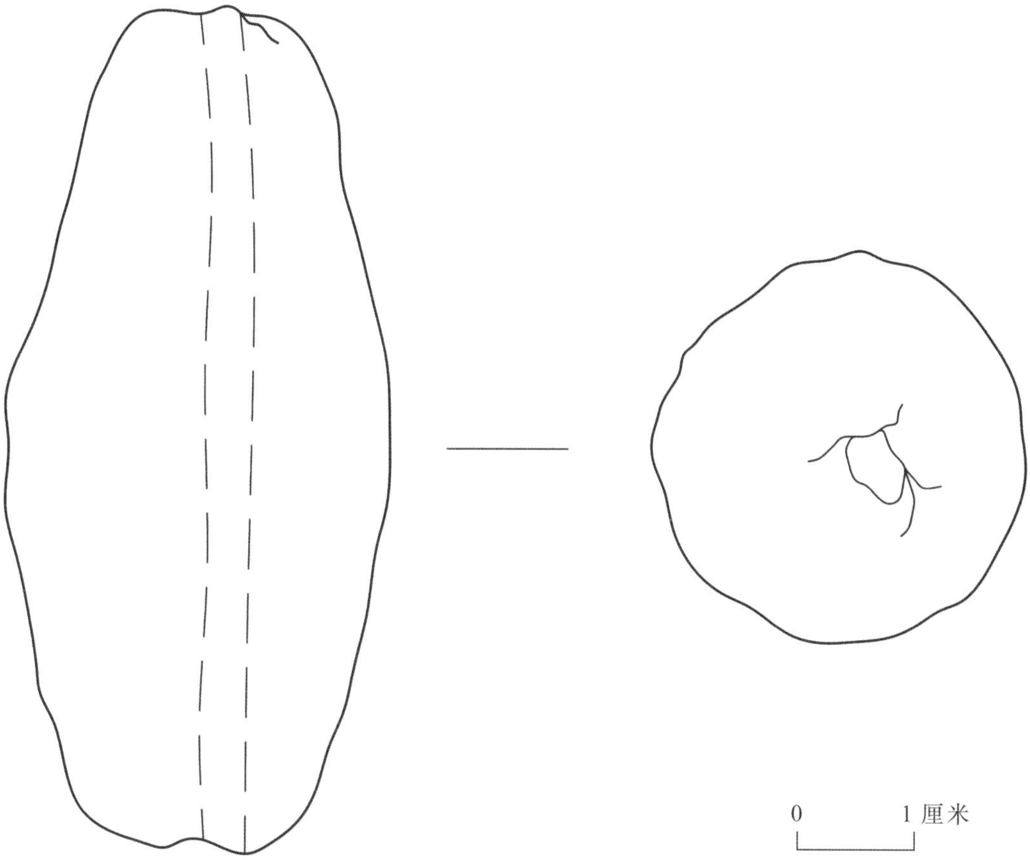

018　陶网坠

Pottery Net Pendant

良渚

月城遗址采集

直径 3.3 厘米、长 6.4 厘米

泥质红陶质。橄榄形，内部有穿孔，素面。

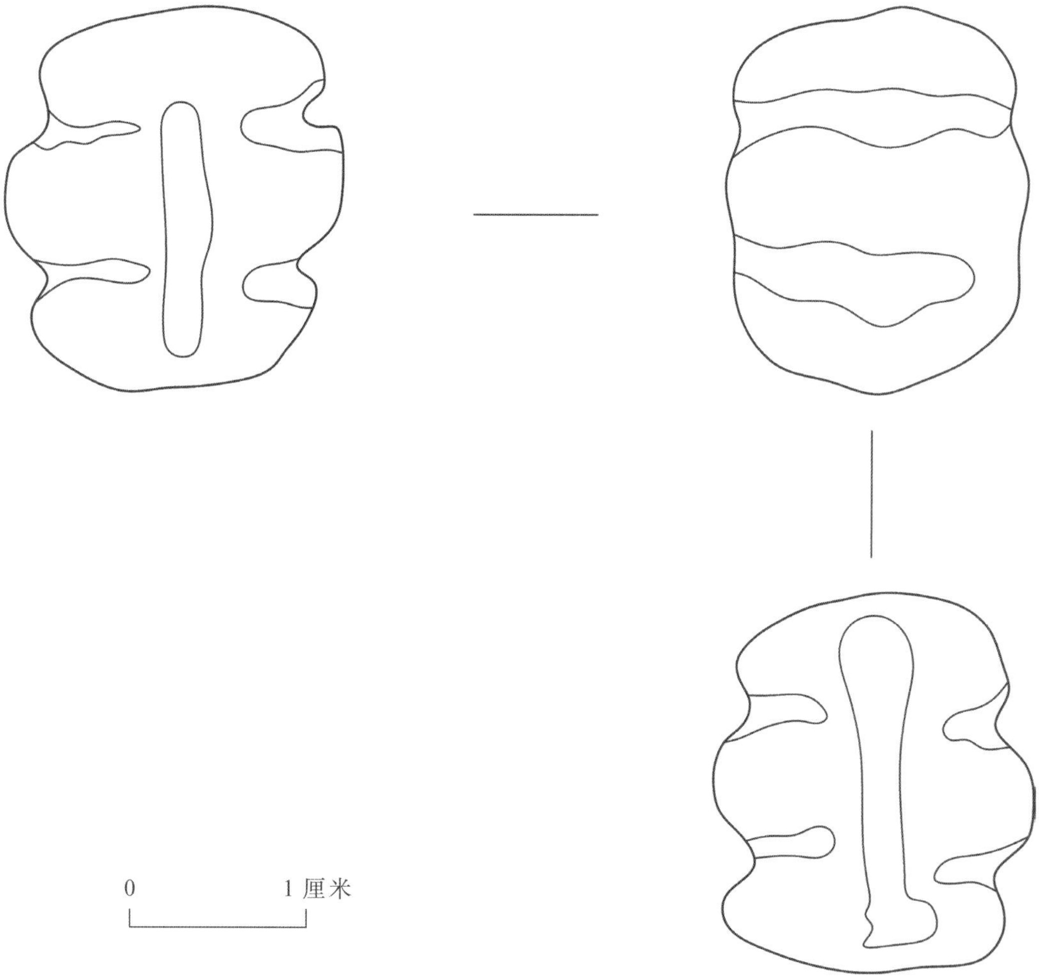

019　陶网坠
Pottery Net Pendant

良渚
月城遗址采集
长 2.1 厘米、长 2 厘米

夹砂红陶质。器身近似圆柱形，两端及两侧各有一道凹槽。

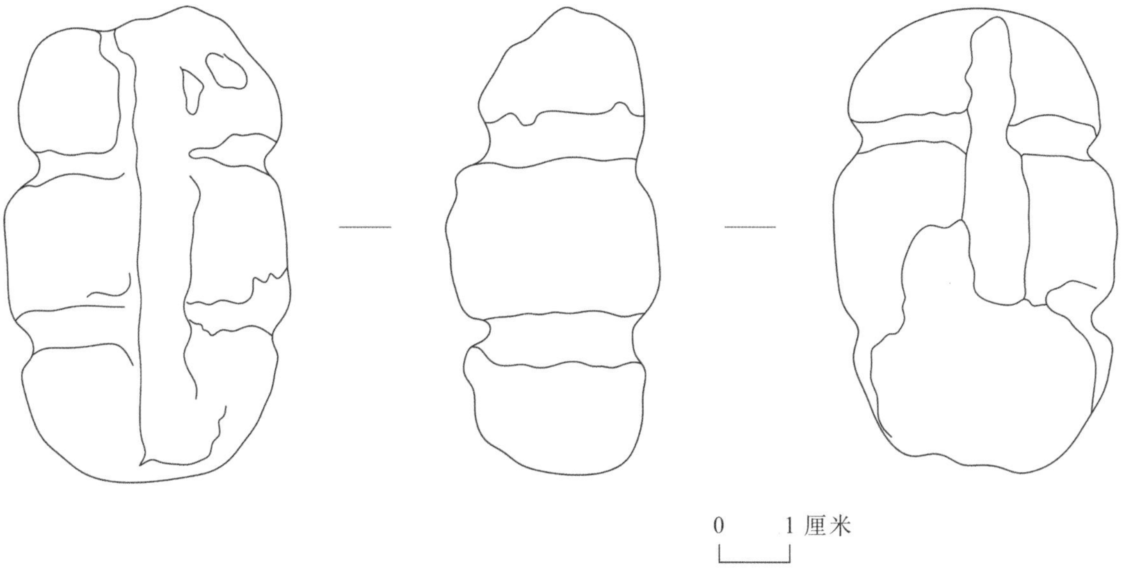

020 陶网坠
Pottery Net Pendant

良渚
月城遗址采集
宽 3.9 厘米、长 5.9 厘米

夹砂红陶质。器身扁圆形，两端及两侧各有一道凹槽。

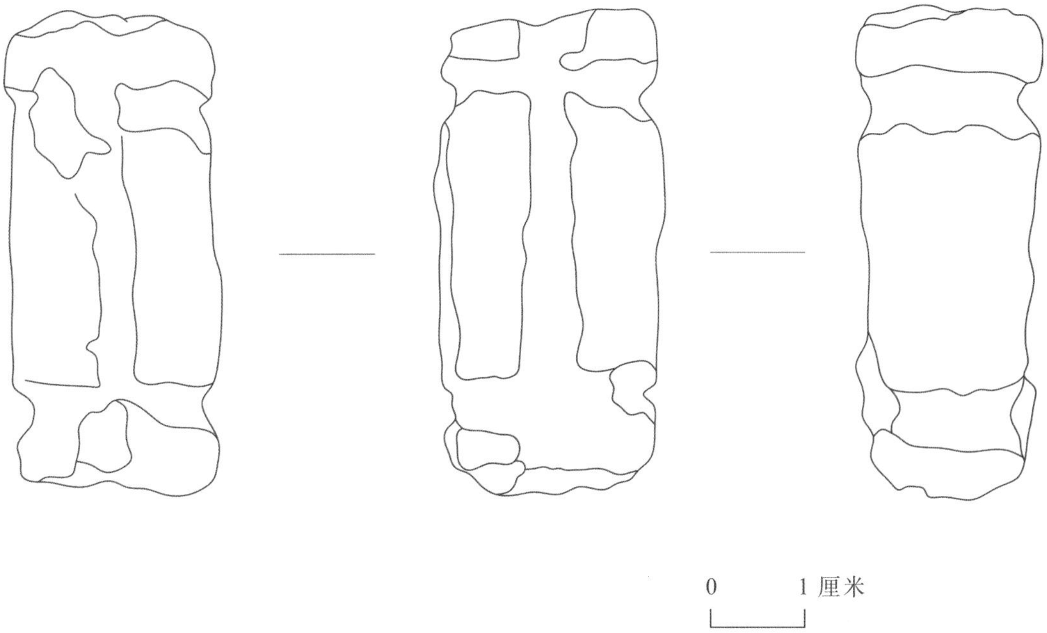

021 陶网坠
Pottery Net Pendant

良渚
月城遗址采集
长 4.7 厘米、宽 2.3 厘米

夹砂红陶质。器身近似长方体形，两端及两侧各有一道凹槽。

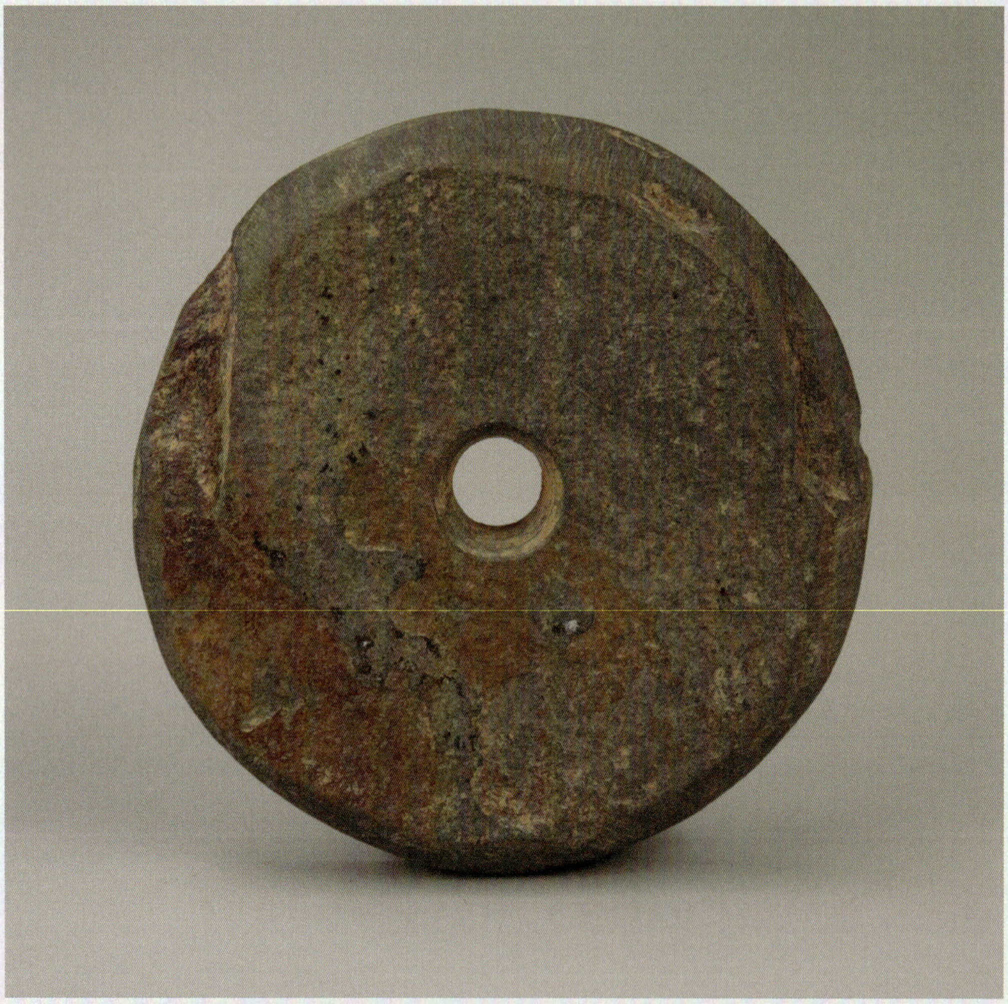

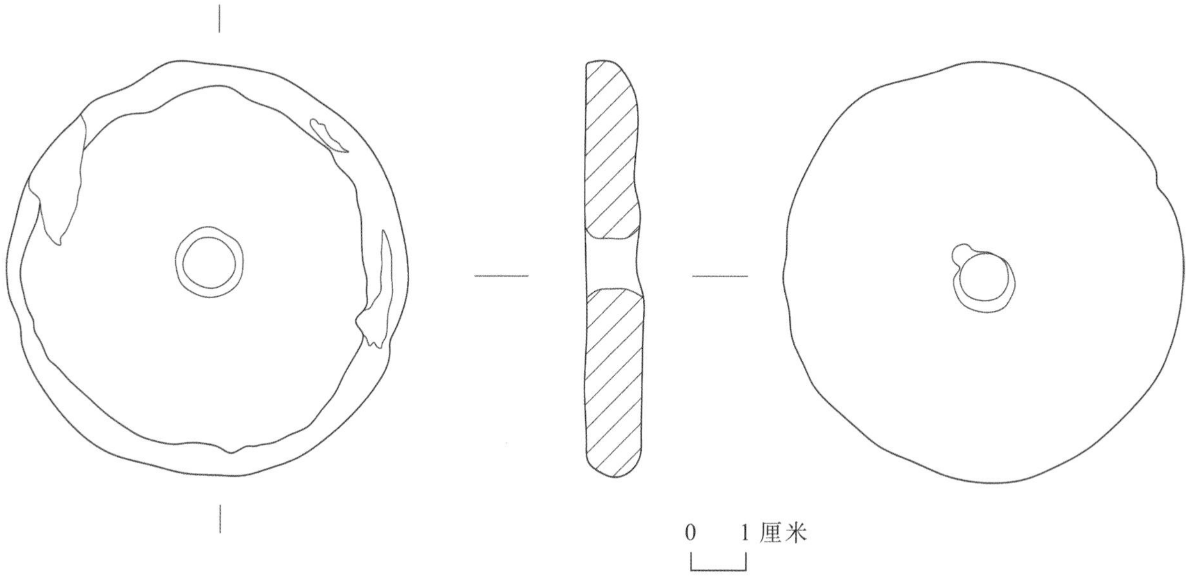

022　石纺轮
Stone Spinning Wheel

良渚
月城遗址采集
直径 7.4 厘米、厚 1 厘米

青石质。圆饼形，扁薄。两面平整，中心有圆形对钻孔。磨制较光滑。

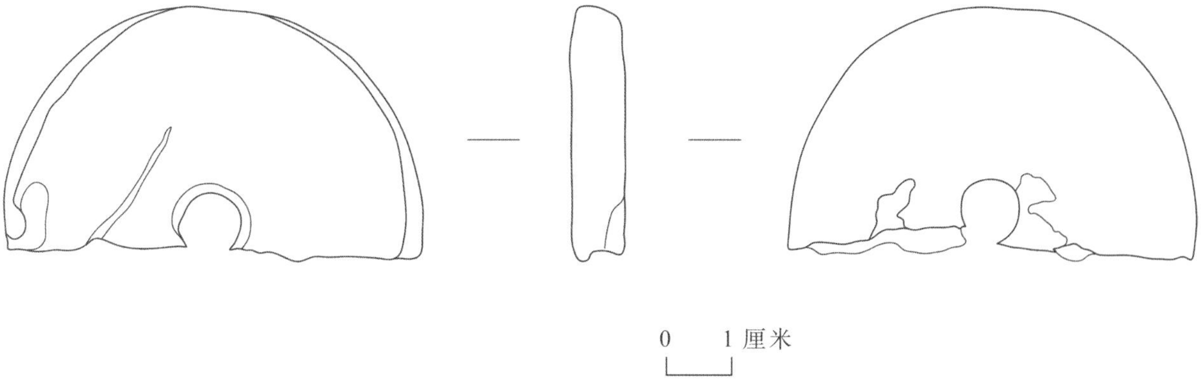

023 石纺轮

Stone Spinning Wheel

良渚

月城遗址采集

复原直径 6.4 厘米、厚 1 厘米

石质。圆饼形，残缺一半，扁薄。两面平整，中心有圆形对钻孔。磨制光滑。

024　陶纺轮
Pottery Spinning Wheel

良渚
月城遗址采集
直径 3.4 厘米、高 1.8 厘米

夹砂灰陶质。器身似轮形，两端面略小，平整，中心有圆形穿孔，腹部较大，有凸棱。

025　陶纺轮
Pottery Spinning Wheel

良渚

月城遗址采集

直径 3.6 厘米、高 2.3 厘米

夹砂红陶质。似扁球形，两面弧凸，腹部直径较大，中心有圆形穿孔。

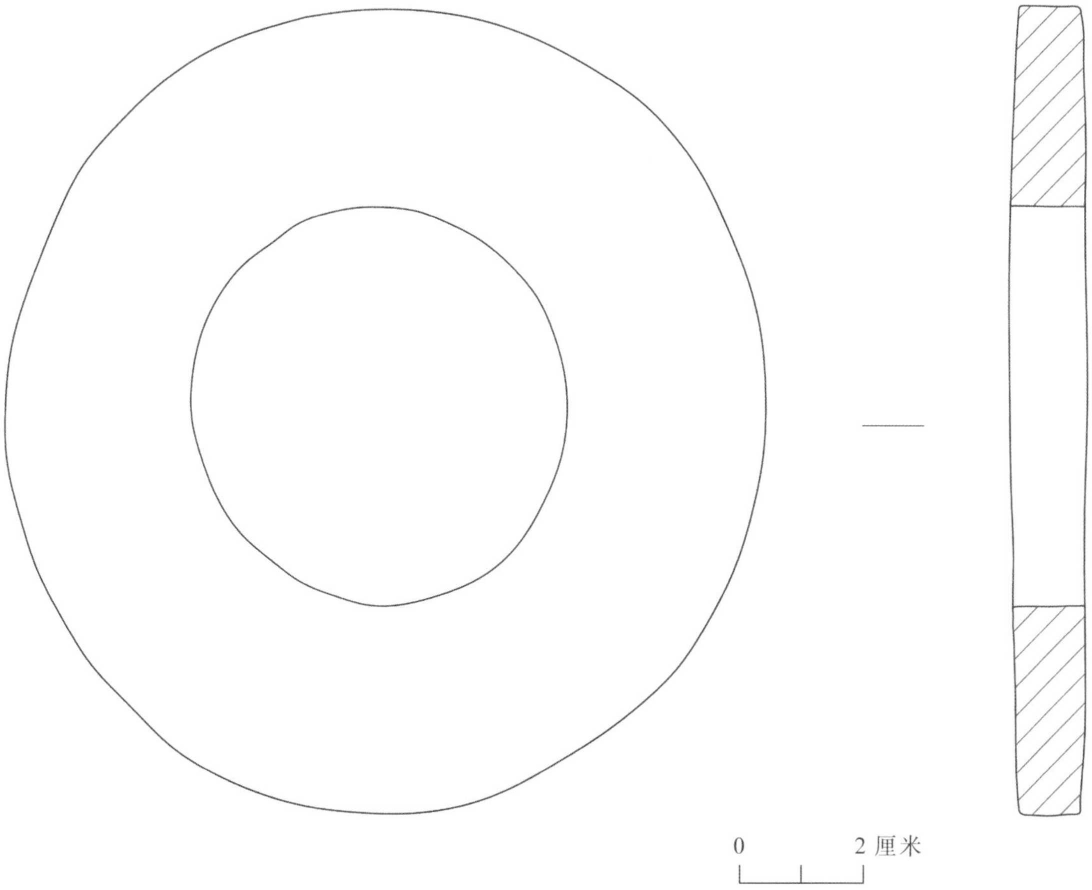

026 玉环
Jade Ring

良渚

月城遗址采集

外径 12.3 厘米、内径 6.3 厘米、壁厚 1.3 厘米

玉质。圆环形，扁平，光素无纹，色泛白。

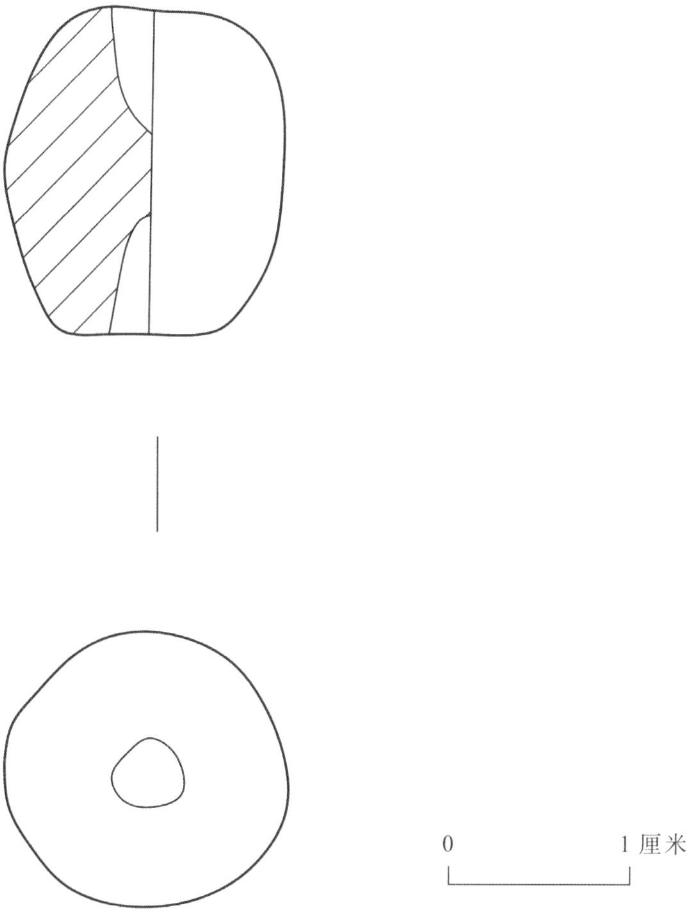

027　玉珠

Jade Bead

良渚

月城遗址采集

腹径 1.5 厘米、高 1.6 厘米

玉质。腰鼓形，两端磨平，腹部上下对穿孔，素面抛光，色泛白。

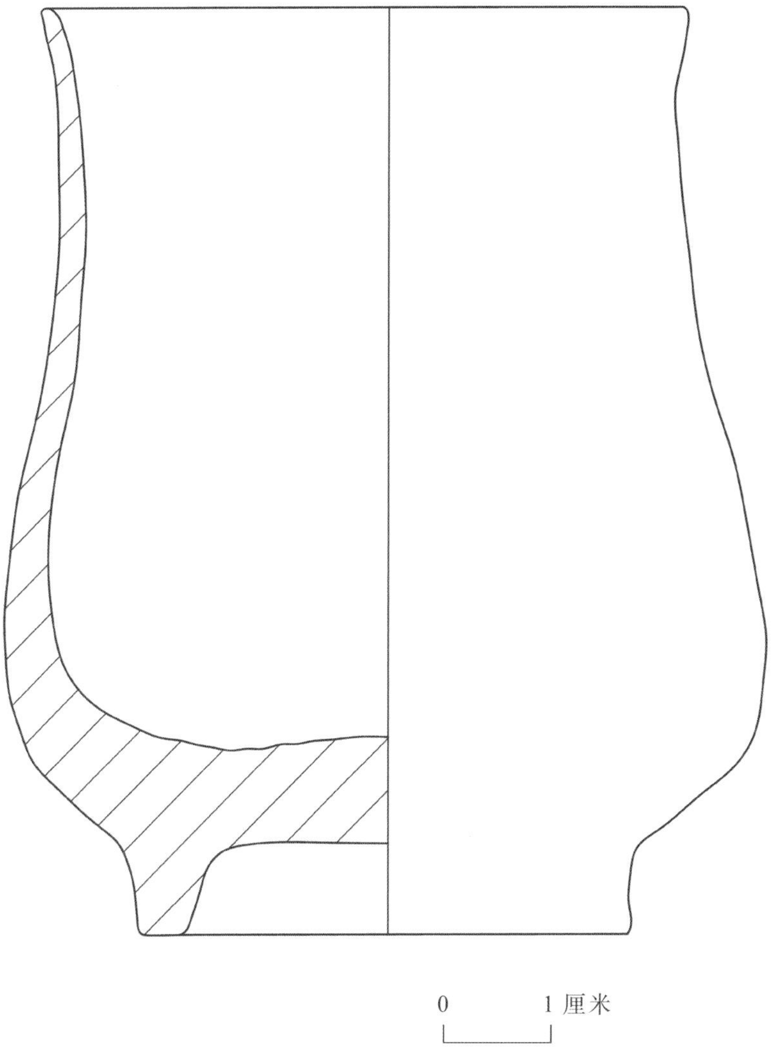

028　陶杯
Pottery Cup

良渚

月城遗址采集

口径 5.2 厘米、底径 4.4 厘米、高 8 厘米

夹砂灰陶质。侈口，垂腹，圈足。素面。

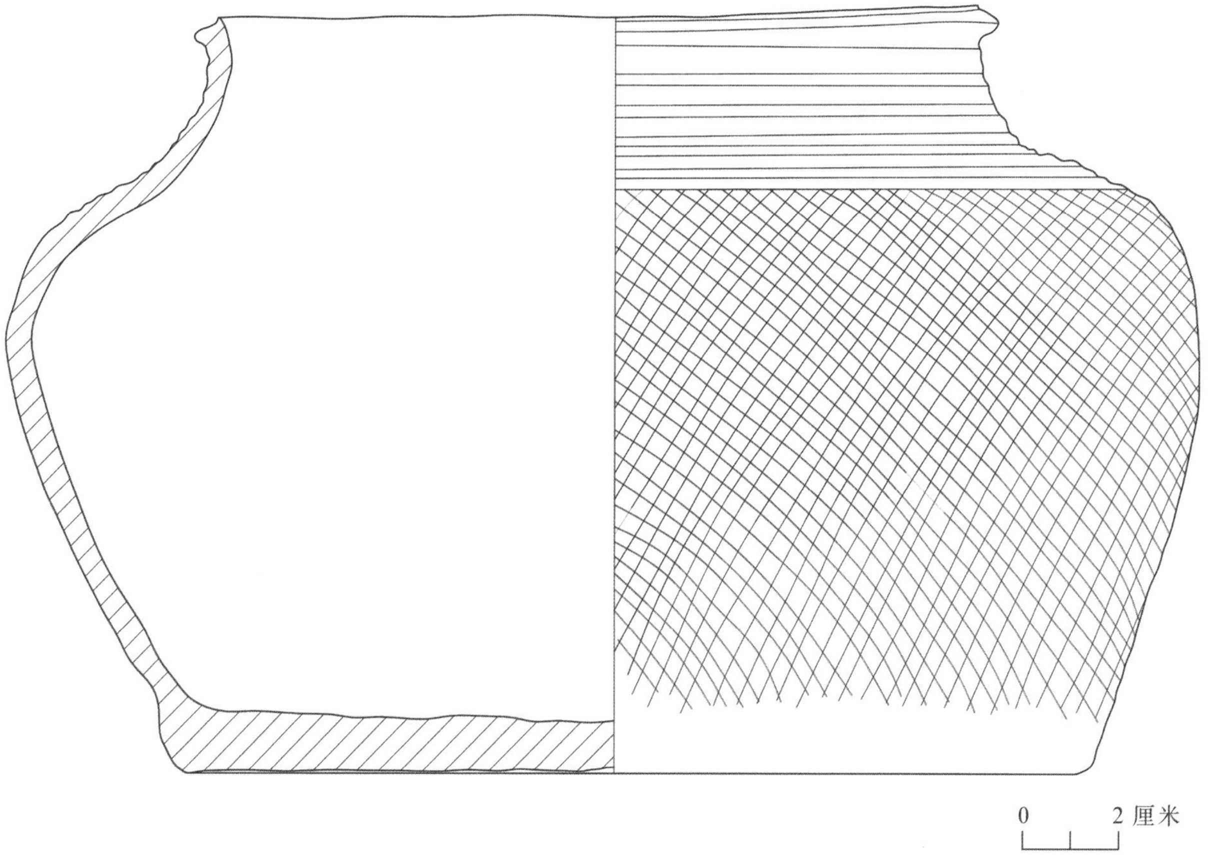

029　陶罐
Pottery Jar

春秋

月城遗址采集

口径 14.4 厘米、底径 18.4 厘米、最大腹径 24.4 厘米、高 15.1 厘米

夹砂硬陶质。侈口，外斜沿略内凹，尖唇，短颈，折肩，鼓腹，平底略有凹凸。颈部和肩部有多组弦纹，腹部满饰方格纹。

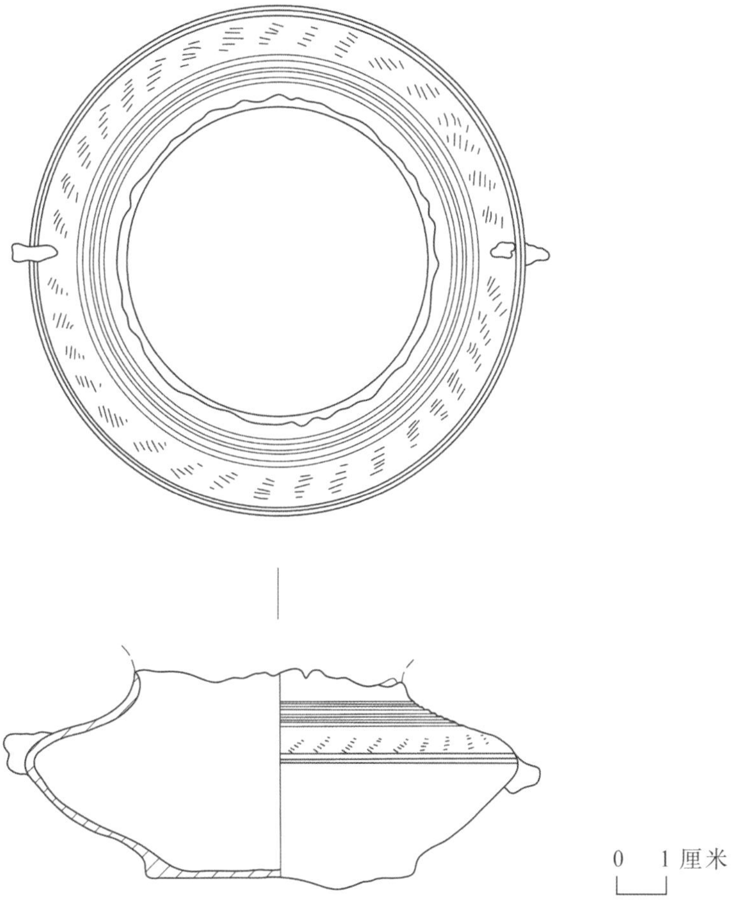

030 陶罐
Pottery Jar

春秋
月城遗址采集
口径6.5厘米、底径5厘米、最大腹径9.7厘米、高3.6厘米

夹砂硬陶质。侈口，尖唇，短颈，平肩，折腹，下腹斜收，似饼足，底平略有凹凸。肩部贴饰双耳，另装饰两组弦纹、一组点纹。

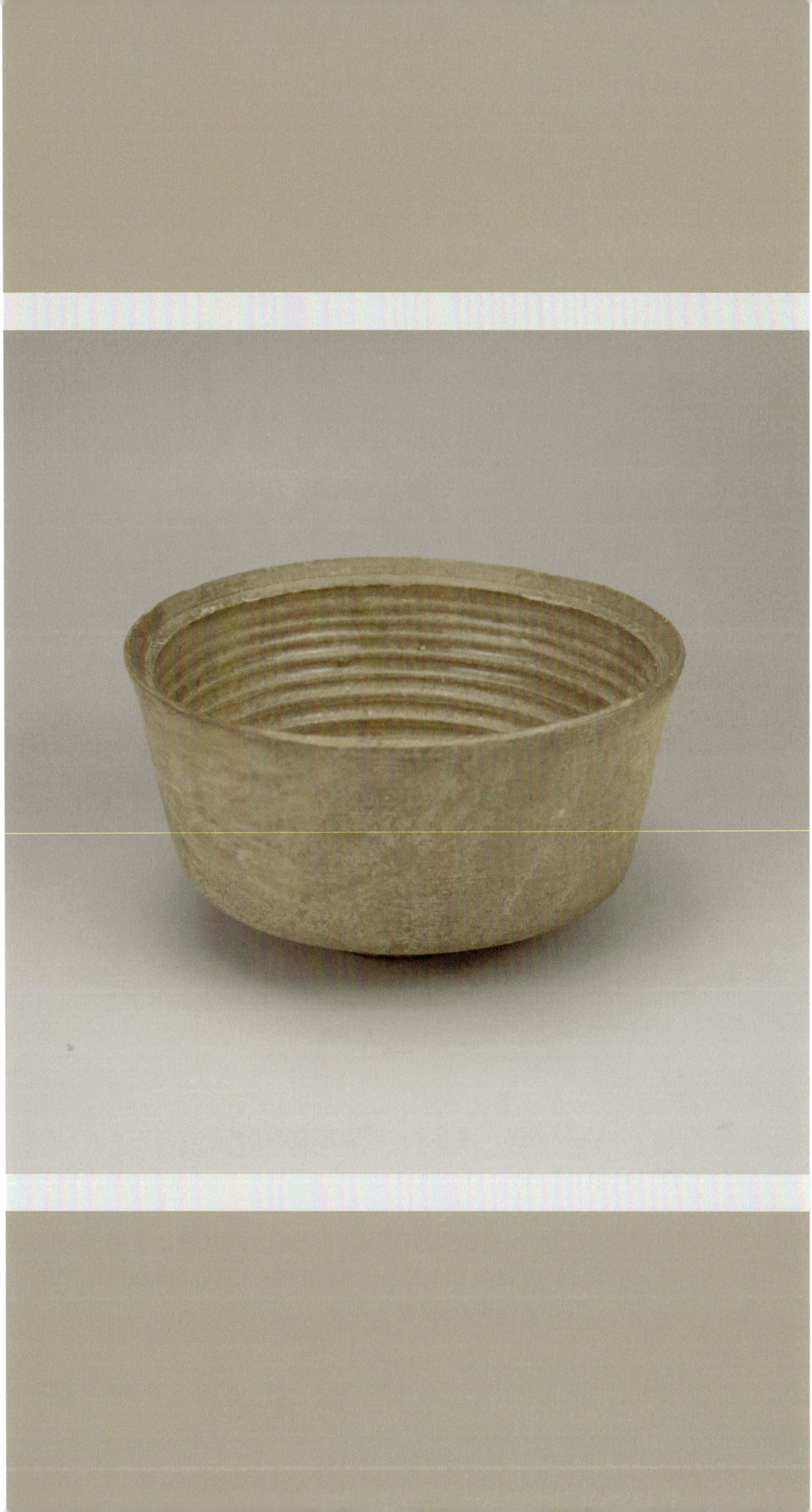

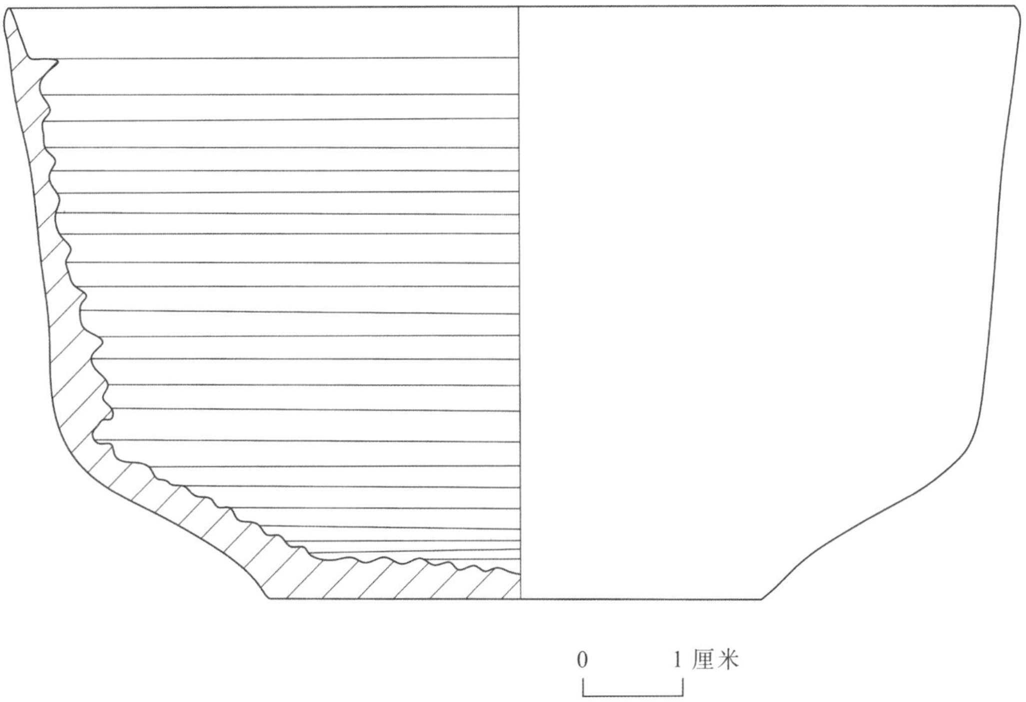

031　原始瓷盅
Proto-Porcelain Cup

春秋
月城遗址采集
口径 10.5 厘米、底径 10.8 厘米、高 5.8 厘米

原始瓷质。侈口，尖唇，斜腹，下腹内折，饼足。口内有台阶，似子母口，内壁满饰凹凸旋纹。内外施青釉，外壁脱釉严重。

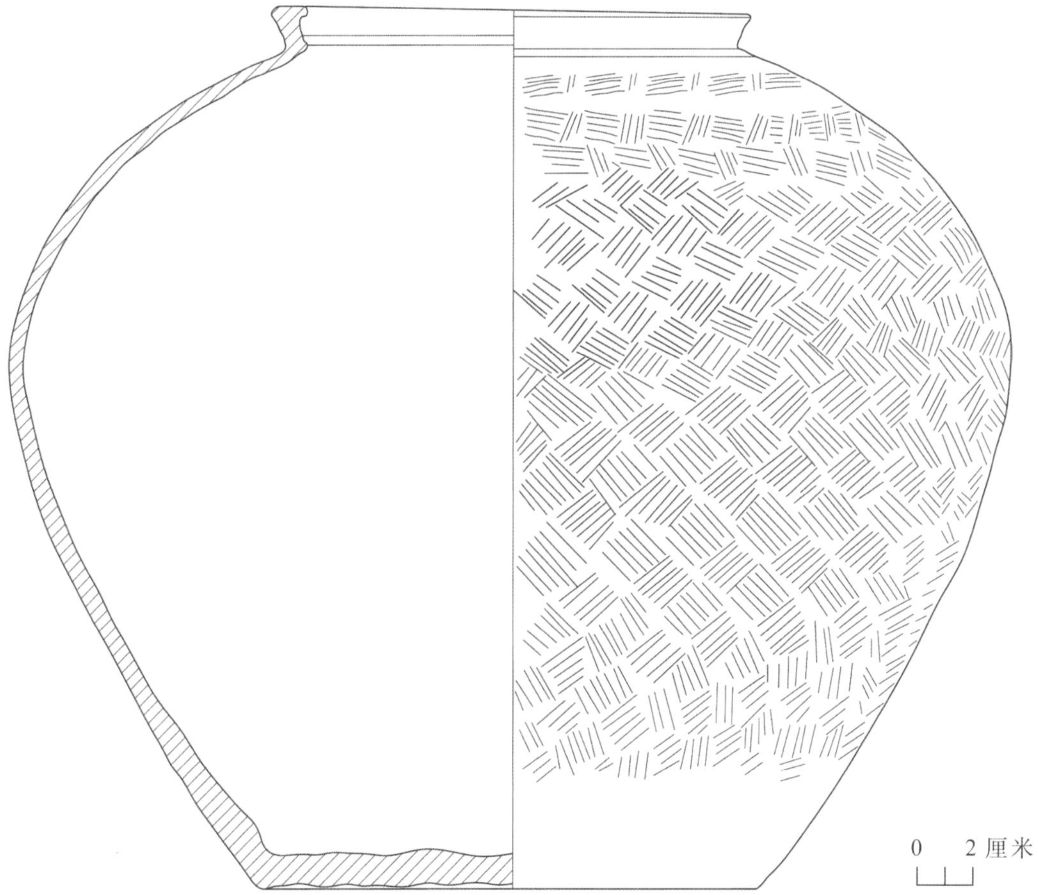

032 陶罐
Pottery Jar

春秋战国

月城遗址采集

口径 14.8 厘米、底径 18 厘米、最大腹径 36.3 厘米、高 29.9 厘米

夹砂硬陶质。敛口，平沿外斜，短颈，溜肩，鼓腹，下腹斜收，平底略内凹。通体饰席纹。肩部以上施青釉，脱釉严重，下腹及底部无釉。

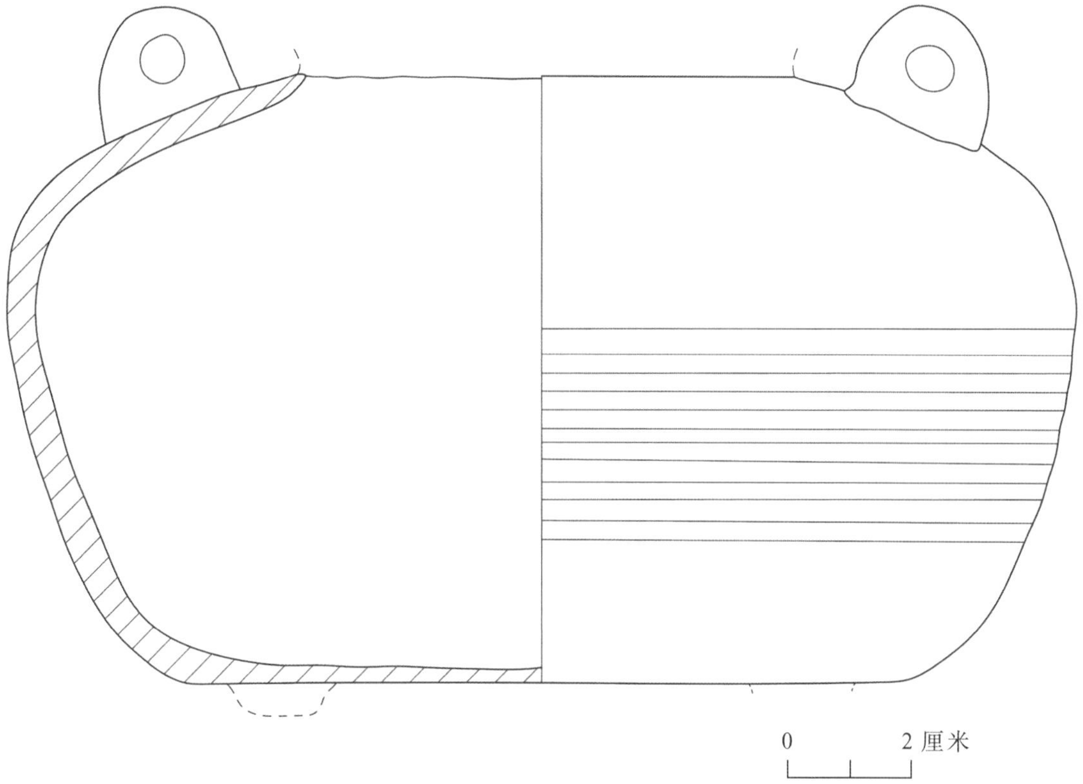

033　陶罐
Pottery Jar

战国

月城遗址采集

底径 11.5 厘米、最大腹径 17 厘米、残高 11.5 厘米

泥质灰陶质。口部残缺，丰肩，鼓腹，平底。肩部贴饰一对拱形耳，底部等距贴饰三个短柱形足。腹部可见多条轮制凹凸弦纹。胎色灰黑，通体磨光。

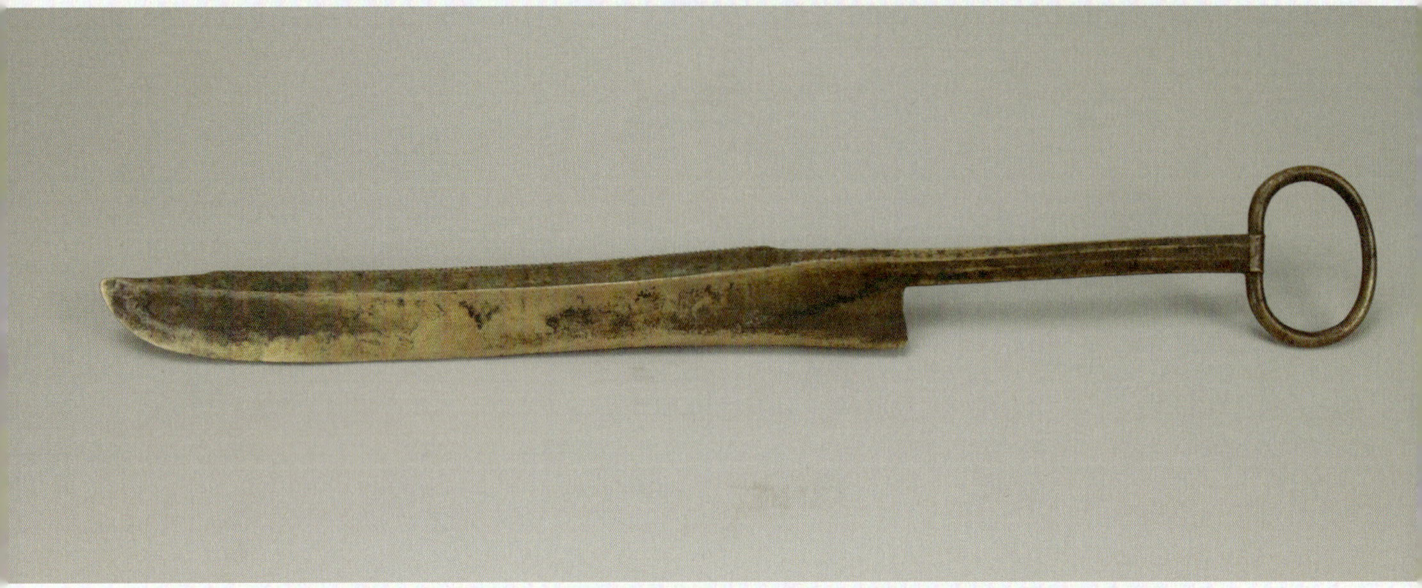

034　铜刀
Copper Knife

战国
稀巷遗址采集
长 26.2 厘米、宽 2 厘米

黄铜质。刀身狭长，柄端有环，刀背窄薄，带锯齿，刀刃亦窄薄，呈流线弧形。

035　铜刀
Copper Knife

战国
稀巷遗址采集
长 18.2 厘米、宽 1.2 厘米

黄铜质。刀身狭长，柄端有环，刀背略宽平，刀刃窄薄。

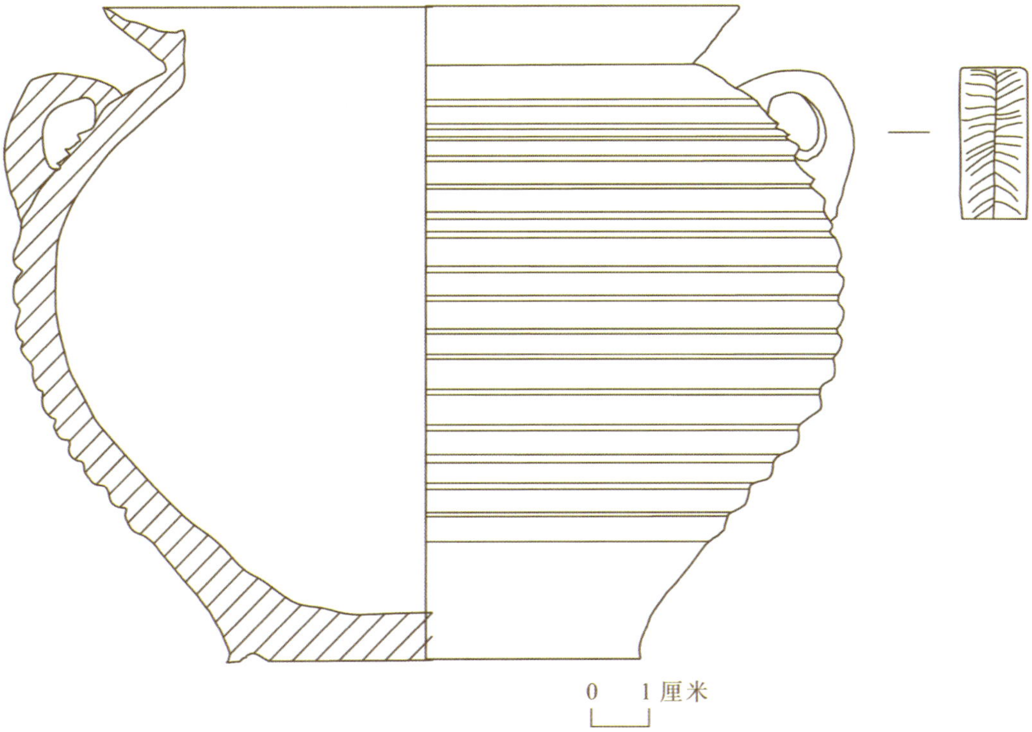

036　陶罐
Pottery Jar

汉

月城遗址采集

口径 8.3 厘米、底径 8.6 厘米、最大腹径 15.8 厘米、高 8.8 厘米

泥质灰陶质。直口，平沿，尖圆唇，短颈，近平肩，鼓腹，下腹斜收，小平底，略内凹。器身可见多条凹凸弦纹。

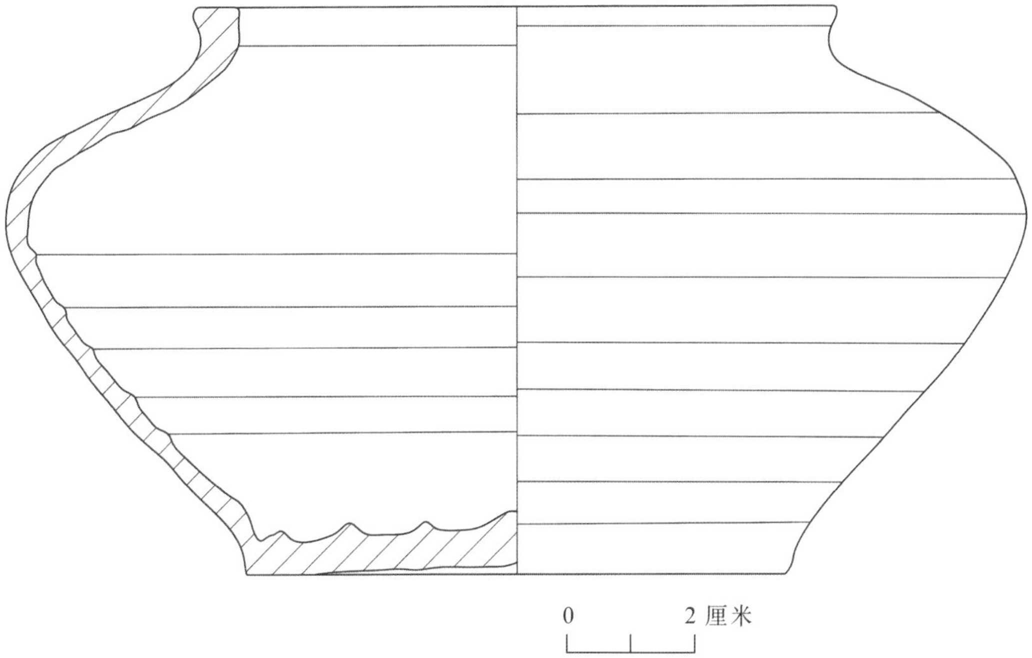

037 陶罐
Pottery Jar

汉

螺蛳墩遗址出土（M8:12）

口径 8.8 厘米、底径 7.2 厘米、最大腹径 15 厘米、高 11.3 厘米

夹砂红陶质。侈口，斜沿，尖唇，短颈，溜肩，鼓腹，下腹斜收，平底略内凹。肩部贴饰一对叶脉纹桥形耳，通体可见多条凹凸弦纹。

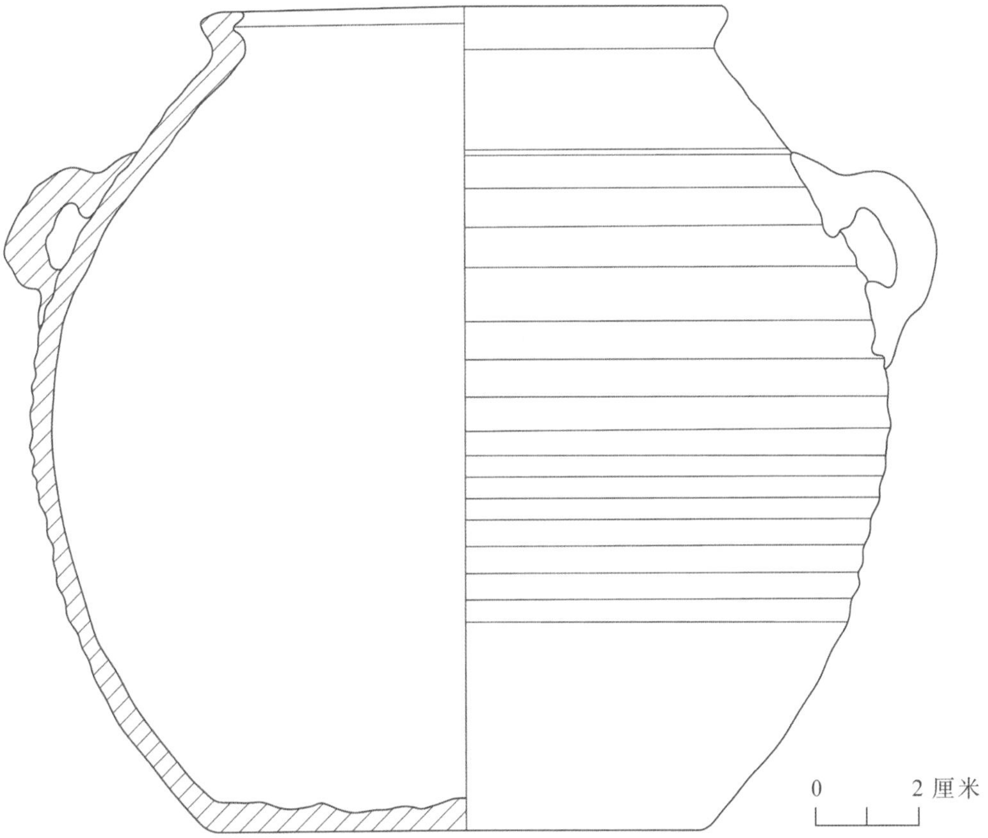

038　陶罐
Pottery Jar

汉

月城遗址出土

口径 8.6 厘米、底径 9.2 厘米、最大腹径 16.5 厘米、高 16 厘米

夹砂红陶质。小口微侈，平沿外折，溜肩，鼓腹，下腹斜收，平底，略内凹。肩部贴饰一对叶脉纹桥形耳，通体可见多条凹凸弦纹。

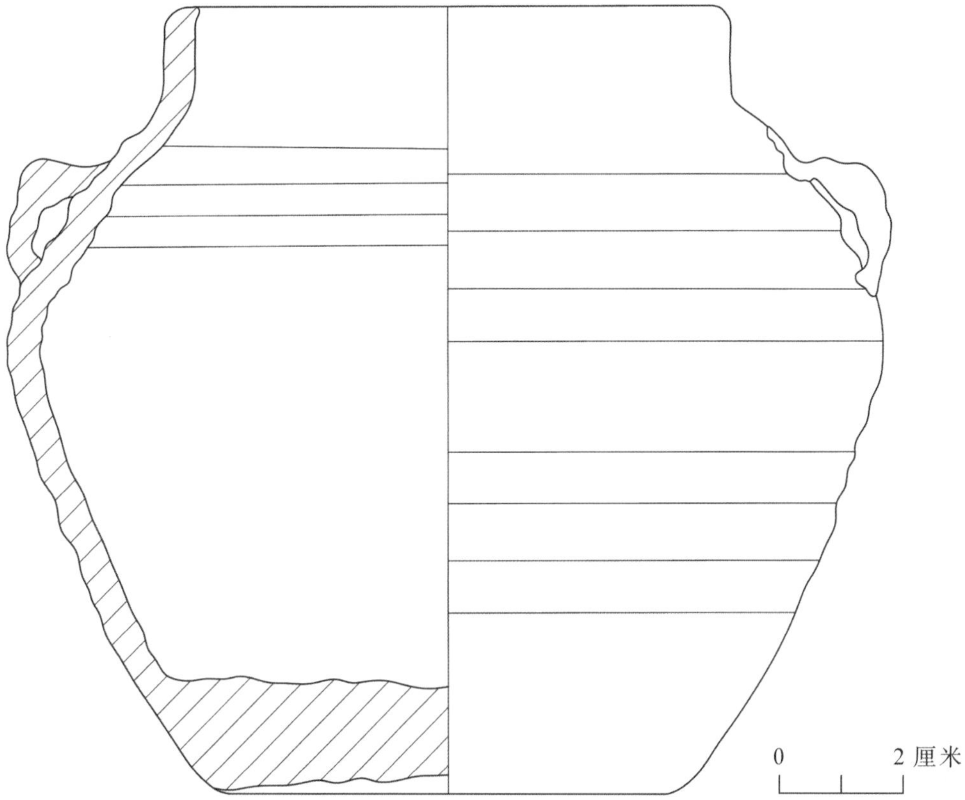

039 陶罐

Pottery Jar

汉

月城遗址采集

口径 7.6 厘米、底径 6.8 厘米、最大腹径 12.4 厘米、高 12.3 厘米

夹砂红陶质。直口，微侈，平沿，略内凹，短颈，溜肩，鼓腹，下腹斜收，小平底，略有凹凸。肩部贴饰一对桥形耳，通体可见多条轮制凹凸弦纹。

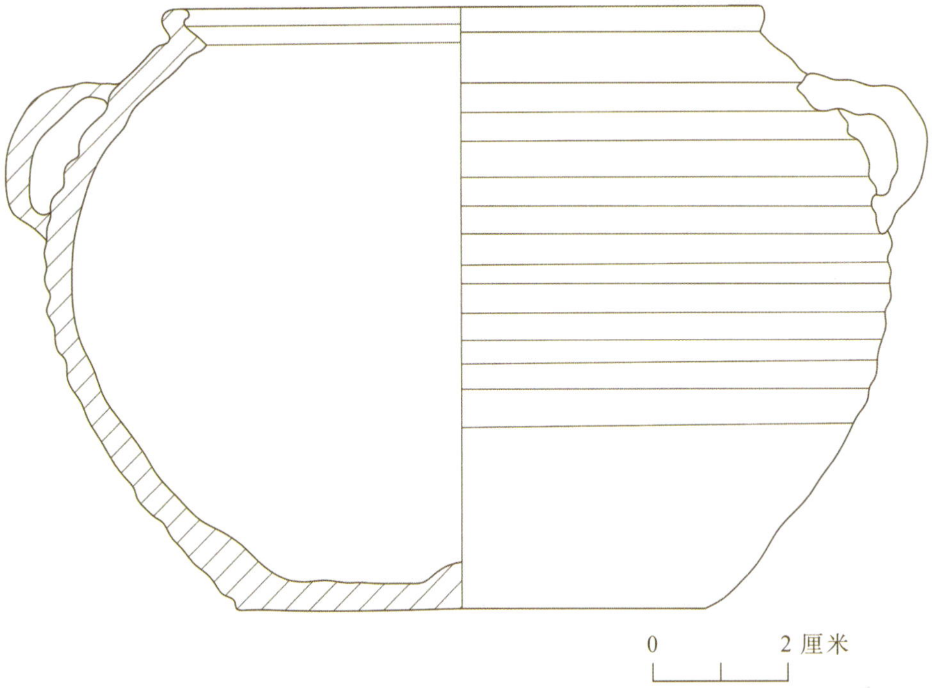

040 陶罐
Pottery Jar

汉

月城遗址采集

口径 7.3 厘米、底径 6.5 厘米、最大腹径 11.9 厘米、高 8 厘米

夹砂灰陶质。小口微敛，沿面内凹，尖圆唇，溜肩，鼓腹，小平底。上腹部贴饰一对叶脉纹桥形耳，器身通体可见多条凹凸弦纹。

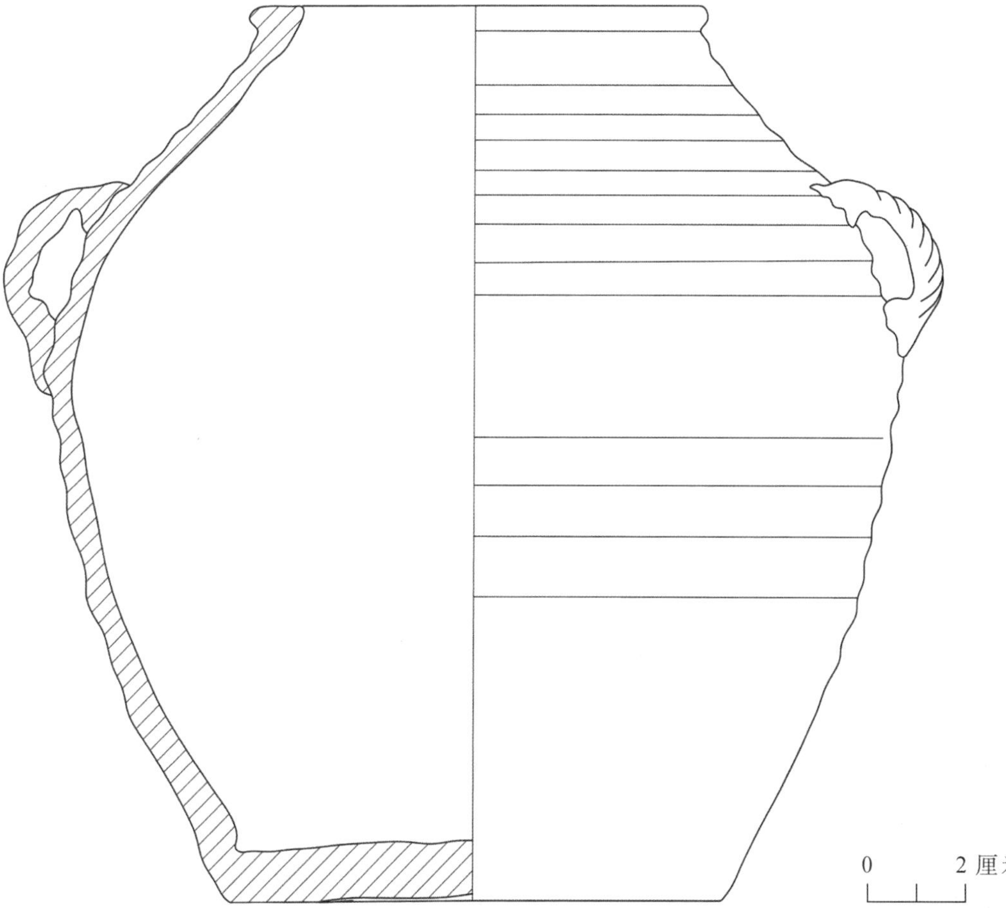

041 陶罐
Pottery Jar

汉

月城遗址采集

口径 8 厘米、底径 10.4 厘米、最大腹径 17.5 厘米、高 17.9 厘米

夹砂灰陶质。小口微敛，平沿外折，尖唇，短颈，溜肩，鼓腹，下腹斜收，小平底，略内凹。肩部贴饰一对叶脉纹桥形耳，通体可见多条轮制凹凸弦纹。

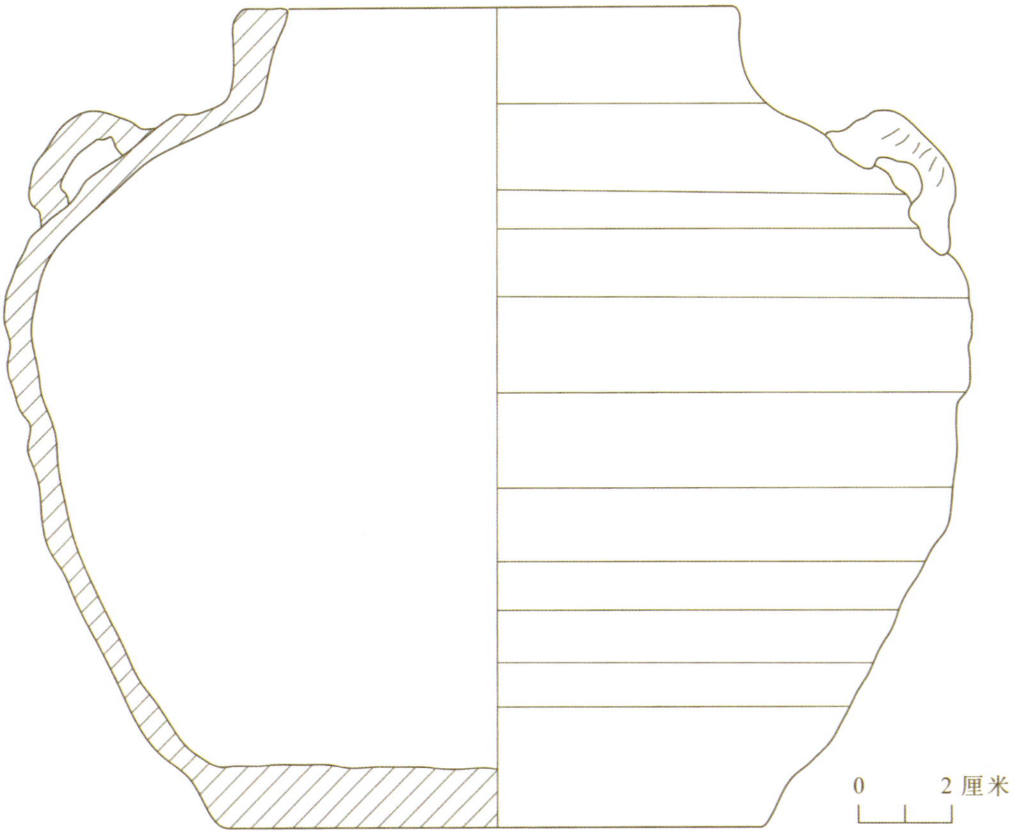

042　釉陶罐
Glazed Pottery Jar

汉

月城遗址采集

口径 8.8 厘米、底径 11 厘米、最大腹径 16.7 厘米、高 17.2 厘米

夹砂灰陶质。小直口，微敛，平沿，略内凹，短颈，溜肩，鼓腹，下腹斜收，平底，亦略内凹。肩部贴饰一对叶脉纹桥形耳，通体可见多条轮制凹凸弦纹。肩部及以上满施青釉，脱釉严重，下腹及底部无釉。

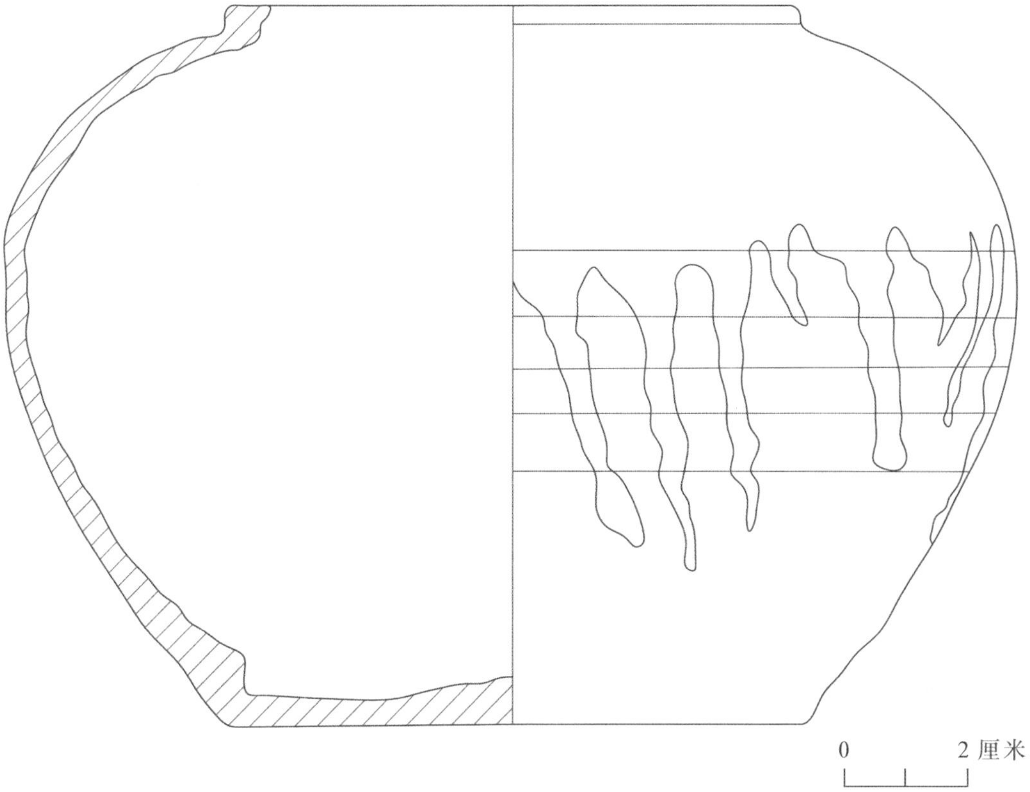

043　釉陶罐
Glazed Pottery Jar

汉

月城遗址采集

口径 8 厘米、底径 9.3 厘米、最大腹径 16.5 厘米、高 11.8 厘米

夹砂灰陶质。微敛口，内斜沿，丰肩，鼓腹，下腹斜收，平底略内凹。素面，器身大部施青釉，多有流釉，下腹及底部无釉。

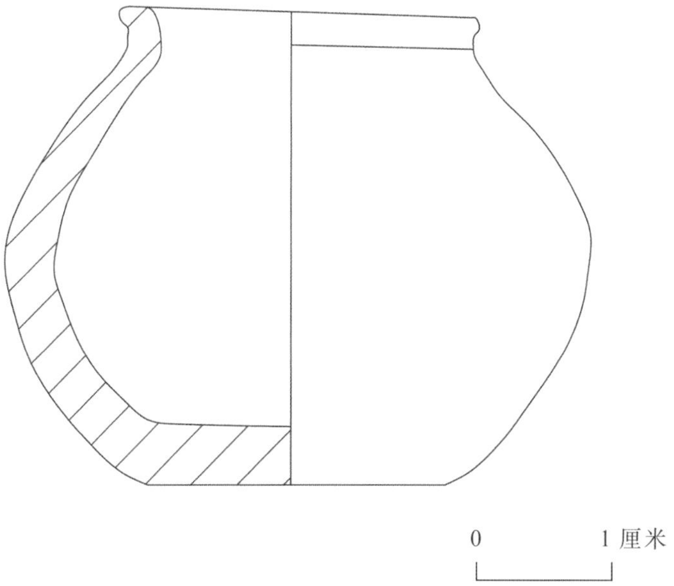

044　釉陶罐
Glazed Pottery Jar

汉

螺蛳墩遗址出土（M16：2）

口径 2.6 厘米、底径 2.5 厘米、最大腹径 4.3 厘米、高 3.2 厘米

夹砂灰陶质。侈口，短颈，溜肩，鼓腹，小平底，略有凹凸。器身上部施青釉，下腹及底部无釉。

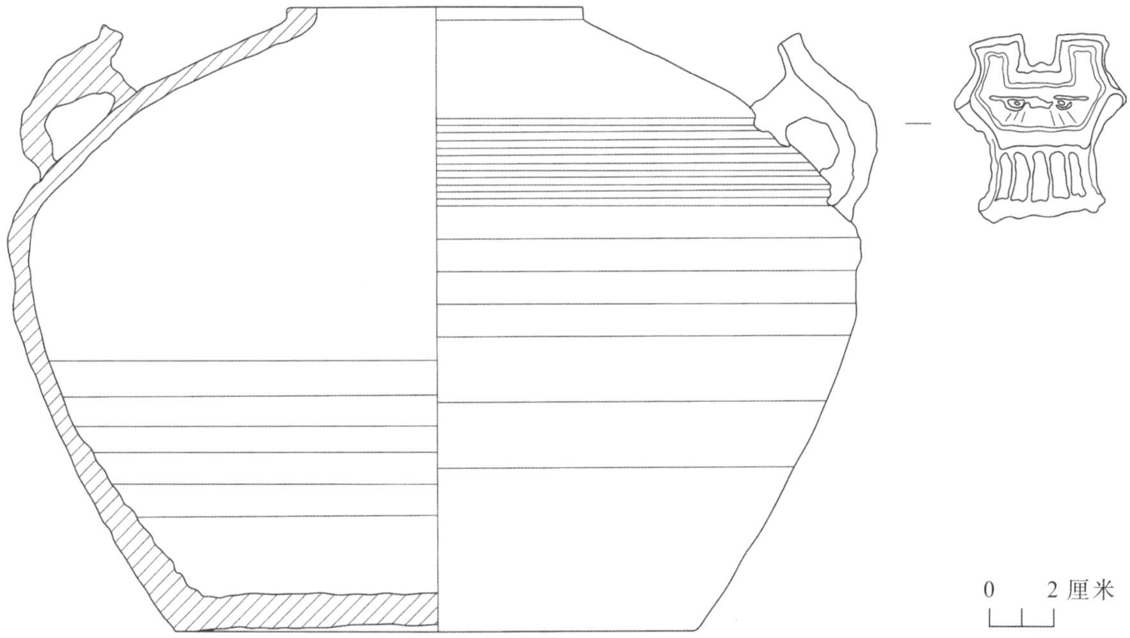

045 釉陶瓿

Glazed Pottery Vase

汉

月城遗址采集

口径 7.5 厘米、底径 16.4 厘米、最大腹径 27.8 厘米、高 19.3 厘米

夹砂灰陶质。小直口，微敛，平沿，略内凹，溜肩，鼓腹，下腹斜收，平底略内凹。肩部贴饰一对兽面耳，通体可见多条轮制凹凸弦纹。肩部以上满施青釉，脱釉严重，下腹及底部无釉，胎质较硬。

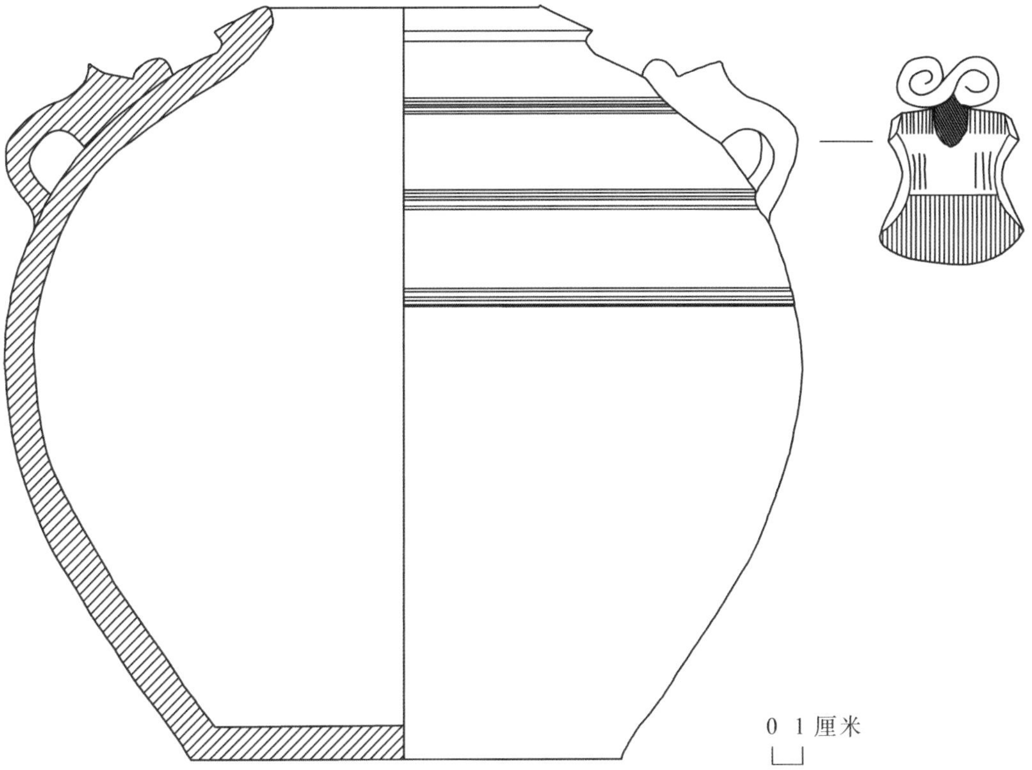

046　釉陶瓿
Glazed Pottery Vase

汉

螺蛳墩遗址出土（M4：1）

内口径8.8厘米、底径14.2厘米、最大腹径26.2厘米、高25厘米

夹砂灰陶质。小敛口，外斜沿，溜肩，鼓腹，下腹斜收，平底内凹。肩部贴饰一对兽面耳，另饰两组凹凸弦纹，腹部饰一组凹凸弦纹，另有多条凹凸较宽不规则弦纹。胎质较硬，夹砂，胎色灰。通体施青釉，脱釉严重，胎质较硬。

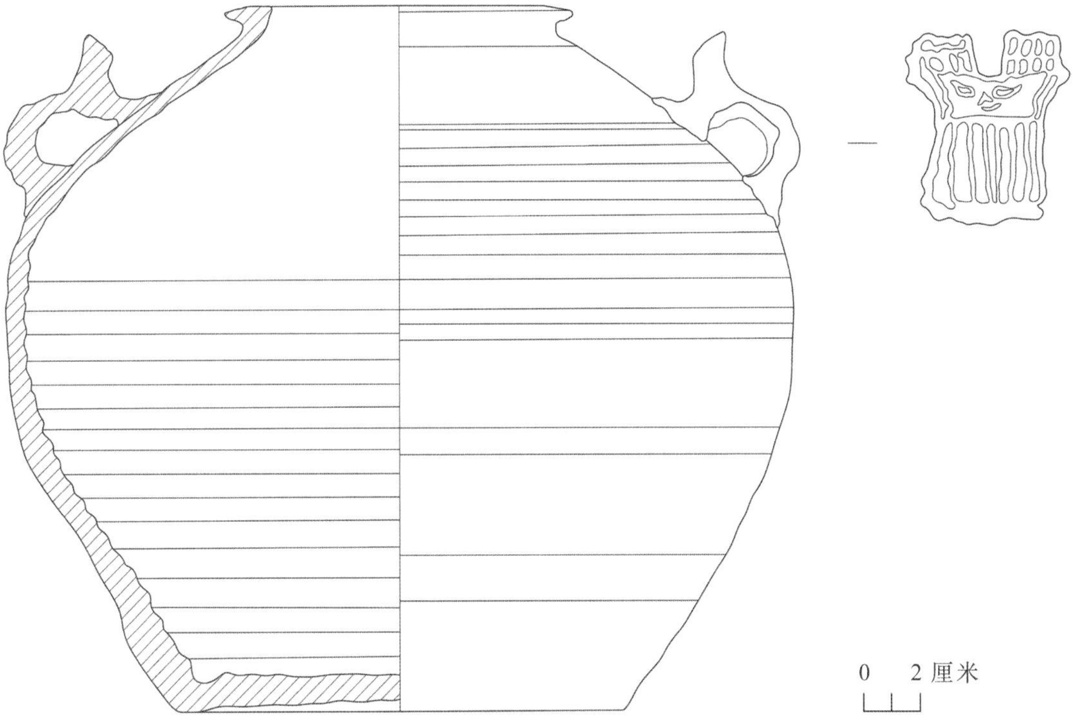

047 釉陶瓿

Glazed Pottery Vase

汉

月城遗址采集

口径 9.6 厘米、底径 12.6 厘米、最大腹径 27 厘米、高 24 厘米

夹砂灰陶质。微敛口，宽平沿，尖唇，短颈，溜肩，鼓腹，下腹斜收，平底内凹。肩部贴饰一对兽面耳，肩部及腹部有多条凹凸弦纹。口沿及肩部施青釉，胎质较硬。

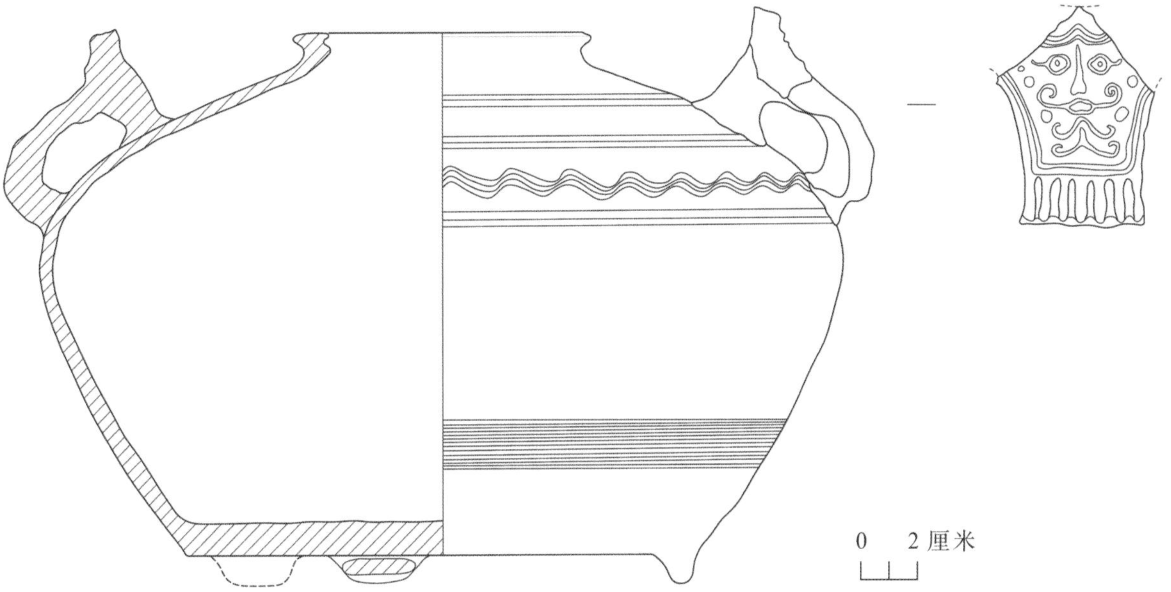

048　釉陶瓿
Glazed Pottery Vase

汉

月城遗址采集

口径 8.7 厘米、底径 17 厘米、最大腹径 27.9 厘米、高 18.9 厘米

夹砂灰陶质。小口微侈，平沿，尖唇，短颈，近平肩，扁鼓腹，下腹斜收，平底，三梯形足。肩部贴饰一对兽面耳。肩部装饰两组水波纹、三足双弦纹。肩部以上施青釉，局部积釉，腹部以下无釉，胎质较硬。

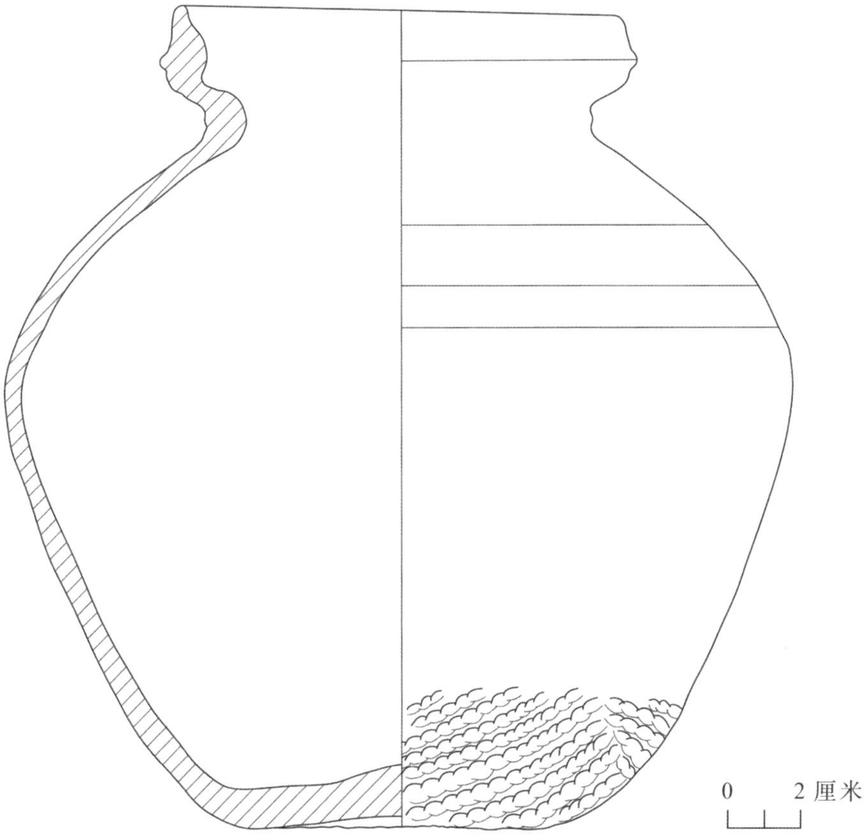

049 陶壶
Pottery Pot

汉

月城遗址采集

口径 12 厘米、底径 7.5 厘米、最大腹径 21.8 厘米、高 23.8 厘米

泥质灰陶质。盘口，尖圆唇，短颈，溜肩，鼓腹，下腹弧收，内凹底。下腹及底部满饰绳纹，其余素面。

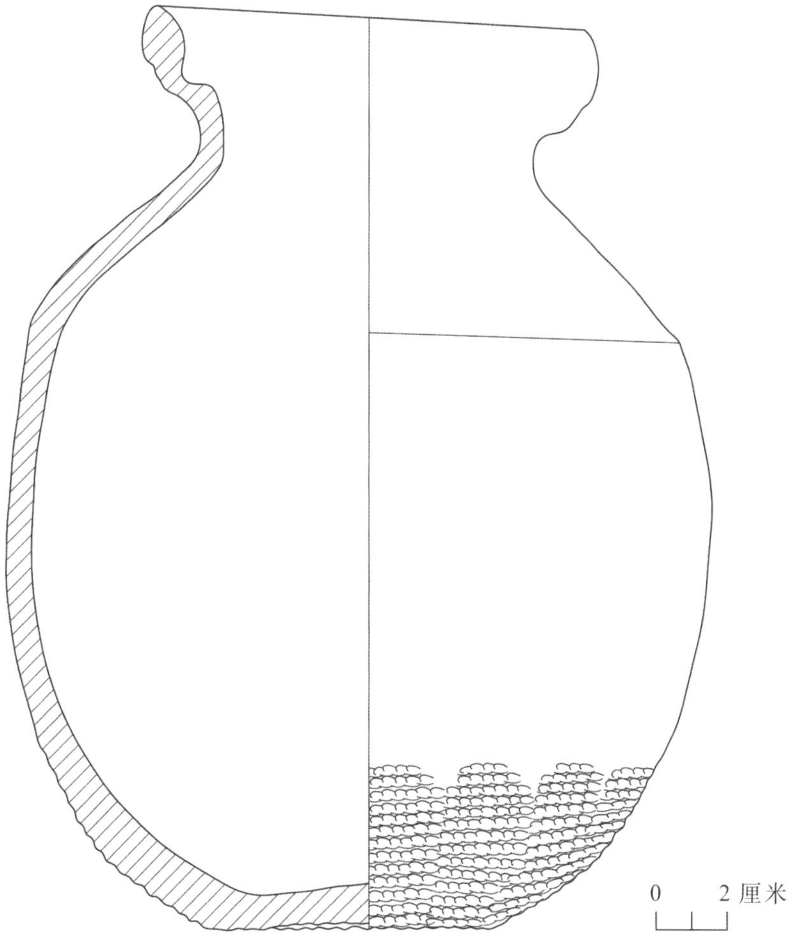

050 陶壶
Pottery Pot

汉

月城遗址采集

口径 12.3 厘米、底径 7 厘米、最大腹径 20.8 厘米、高 25 厘米

夹砂灰陶质。盘口，圆唇，短束颈，斜溜肩，弧腹，近平底，略内凹。下腹及底部满饰绳纹。

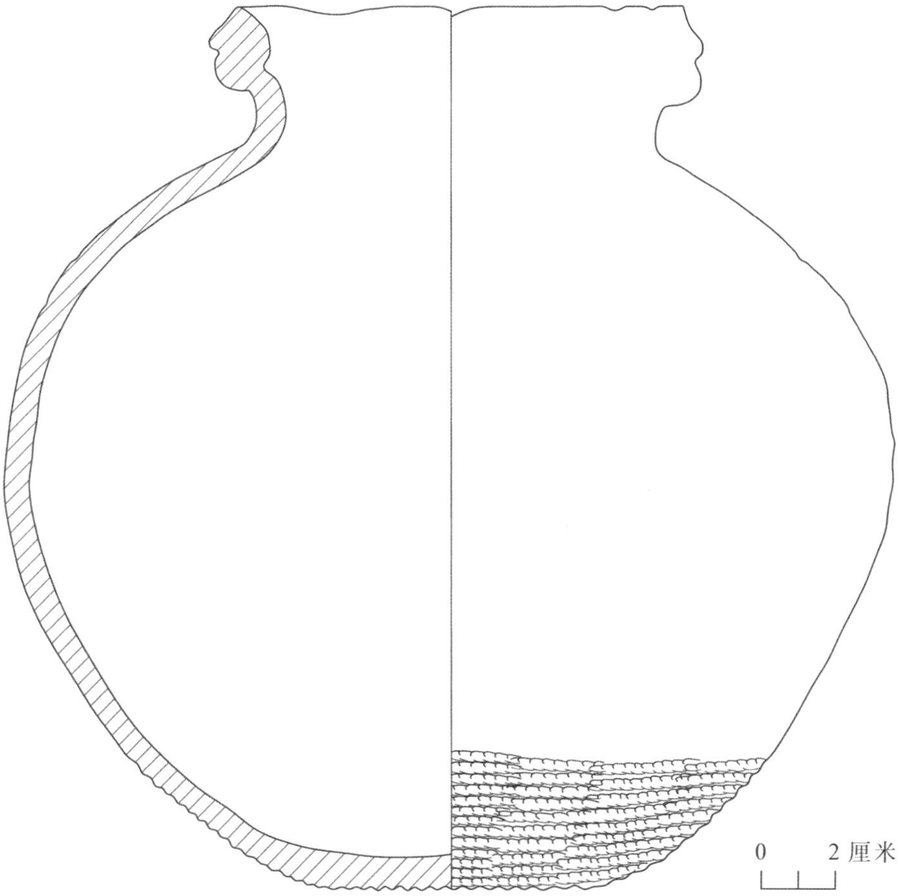

051 陶壶
Pottery Pot

汉

月城遗址采集

口径 15 厘米、底径 7 厘米、最大腹径 24.3 厘米、高 22.8 厘米

夹砂灰陶质。盘口，尖圆双层唇，短颈，溜肩，鼓腹，下腹弧收，近小平底。下腹及底部满饰绳纹，其余素面。

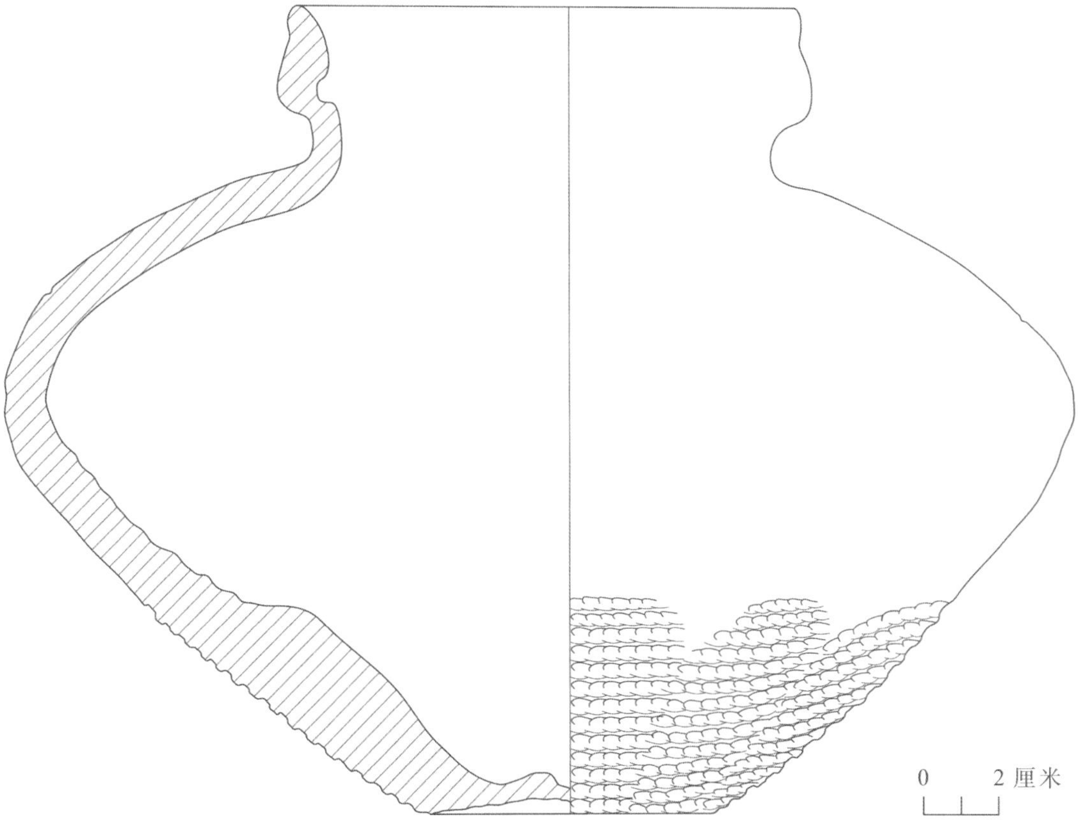

052 陶壶
Pottery Pot

汉

月城遗址采集

口径 13 厘米、底径 7.5 厘米、最大腹径 28.2 厘米、高 20.7 厘米

泥质灰陶质。盘口，圆唇，短束颈，斜肩，扁鼓腹，下腹斜收，小平底，内凹。肩部饰一周凹弦纹，下腹近底部有纵向凸棱，且有多条绳纹填满其间，器壁厚重，胎质较松软。

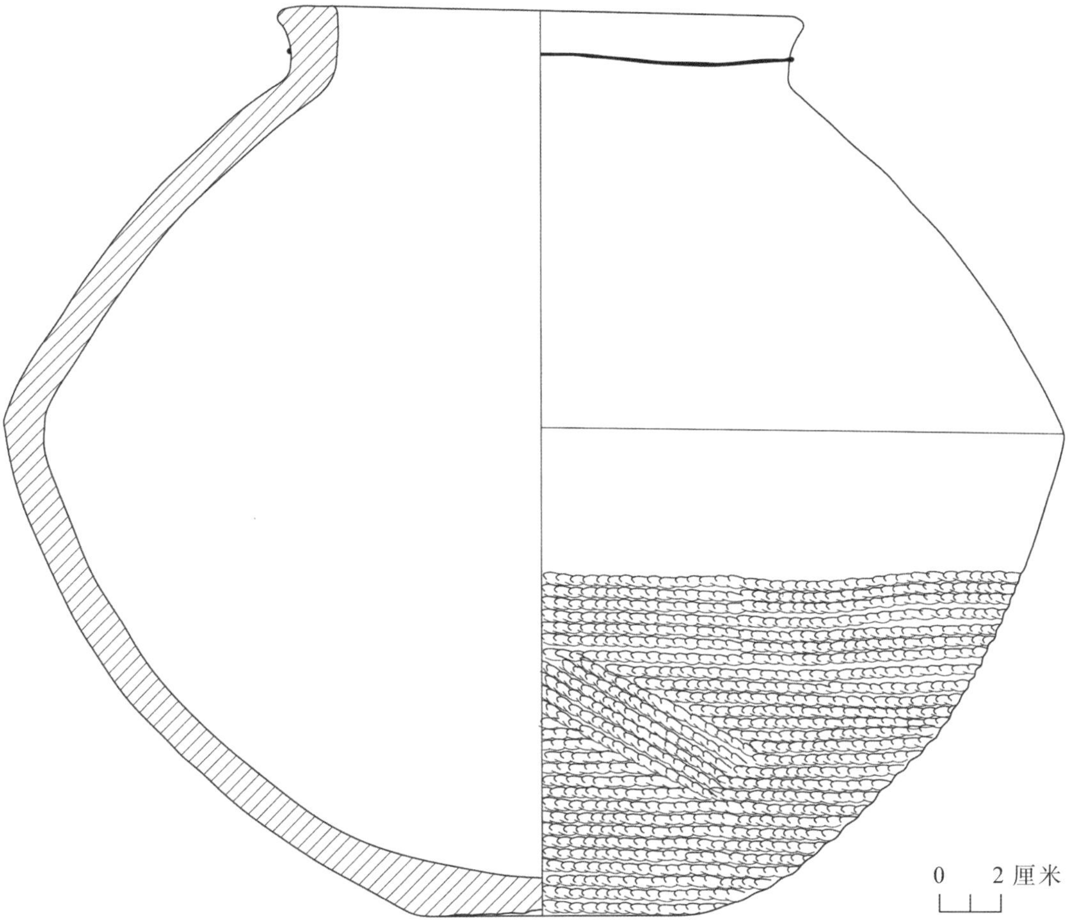

053　陶壶
Pottery Pot

汉

月城遗址采集

口径 13.3 厘米、底径 8.5 厘米、最大腹径 34.5 厘米、高 28.8 厘米

夹砂灰陶质。直口，宽平沿，短颈，斜肩，折腹，下腹斜收，小平底内凹。下腹压印横向绳纹，器壁厚重，胎质较松软。

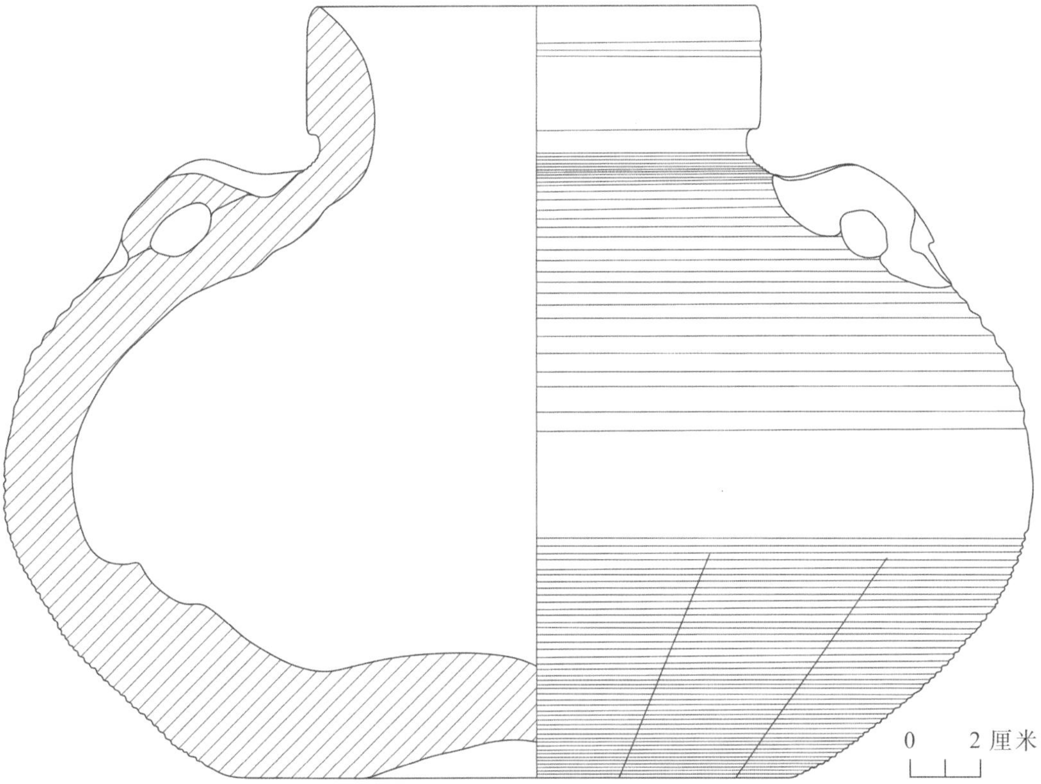

054　陶壶
Pottery Pot

汉
月城遗址采集
口径 12.2 厘米、底径 11 厘米、最大腹径 29 厘米、高 21.5 厘米

夹砂灰陶质。侈口，尖圆唇，短直颈，溜肩，扁鼓腹，下腹斜收，小平底，内凹较深。肩部有一对桥形耳，通体饰凹凸弦纹。器壁厚重，胎质较硬。

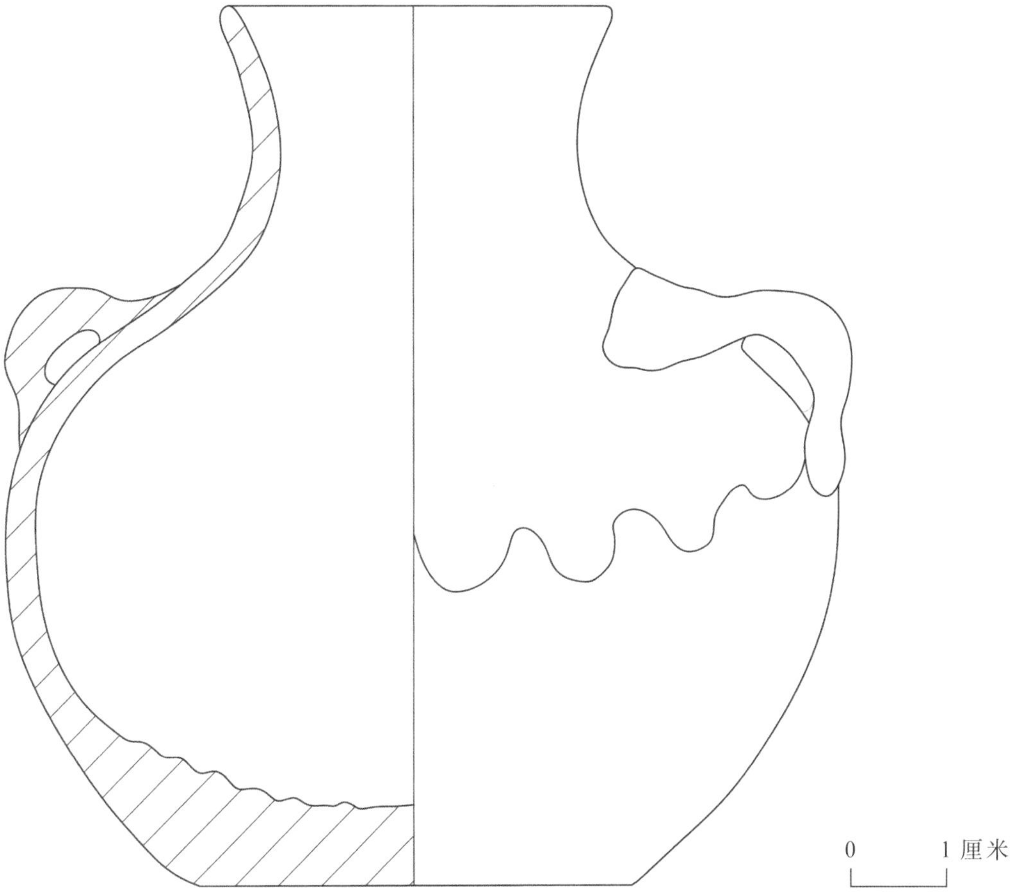

055　釉陶壶
Glazed Pottery Pot

汉

月城遗址采集

口径4厘米、底径4.5厘米、最大腹径8.5厘米、高8.8厘米

夹砂硬陶质。小侈口，束颈，溜肩，鼓腹，小平底。肩部贴饰一对桥形耳。器身上部施青釉，下腹及底部无釉。

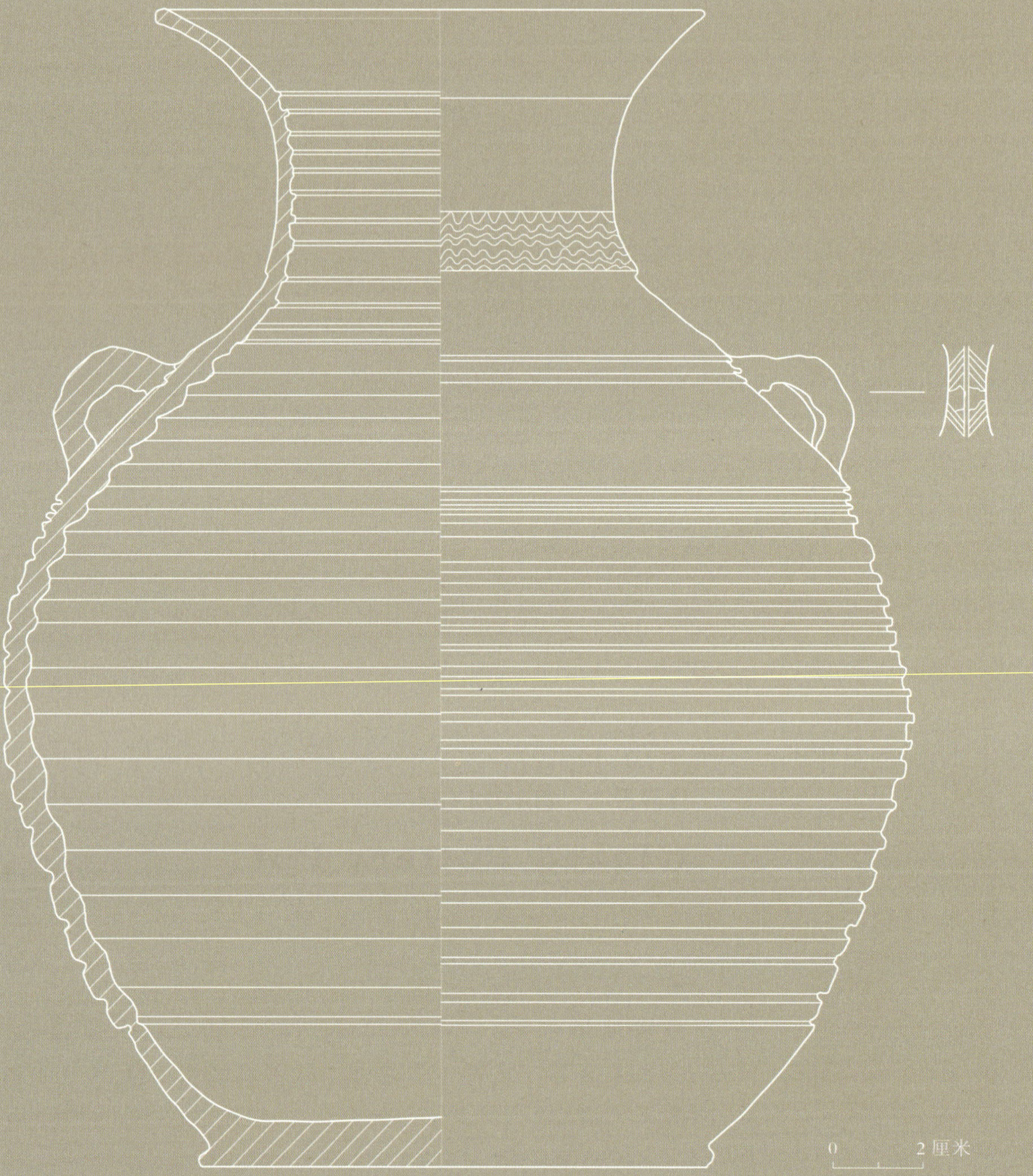
0 2厘米

056 陶壶
Pottery Pot

汉

螺蛳墩遗址出土（M16：12）

口径 12.9 厘米、底径 11.4 厘米、最大腹径 20.6 厘米、高 25.5 厘米

夹砂硬陶质。喇叭口，尖圆唇，束直颈，溜肩，鼓腹，下腹斜收，足不明显，隐圈足。颈部饰一组水波纹，肩部贴饰一对叶脉纹桥形耳，另有两组双凹弦纹，腹部有多条凹凸弦纹。

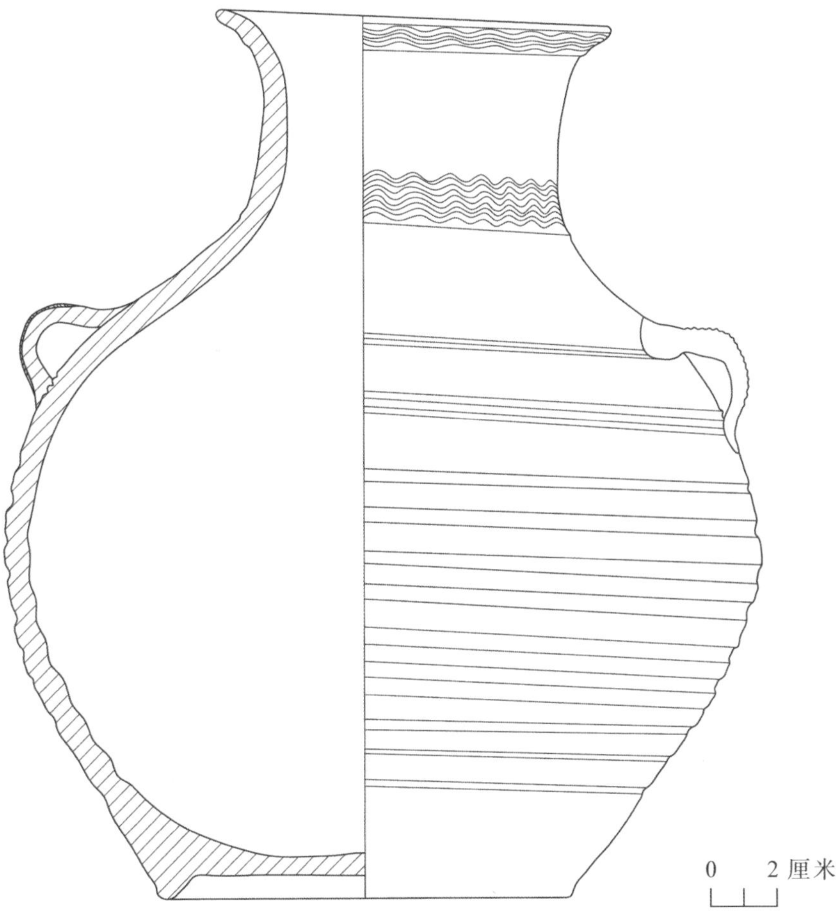

057 釉陶壶
Glazed Pottery Pot

汉

稀巷遗址采集

口径 11.8 厘米、底径 11.8 厘米、最大腹径 22.5 厘米、高 25.7 厘米

夹砂硬陶质。喇叭口，圆唇，束直颈，溜肩，鼓腹，下腹斜收，隐圈足。沿下部和颈部各饰一组水波纹，肩部贴饰一对叶脉纹桥形耳，另有两组凹凸细弦纹，腹部有多条凹凸粗弦纹。上腹施青釉，脱釉严重。

0 1厘米

058　釉陶壶
Glazed Pottery Pot

汉

螺蛳墩遗址出土（M4：3）

口径 9.5 厘米、底径 9.2 厘米、最大腹径 16 厘米、高 22.3 厘米

夹砂硬陶质。喇叭口，平沿，宽唇，束颈，溜肩，鼓腹，下腹斜收，隐圈足。颈部下端饰一组水波纹，肩部贴饰一对“S”形如意纹和叶脉纹桥形耳，肩腹部可见多条凹凸弦纹。器身上部施青釉，脱釉严重，下腹及底部无釉。

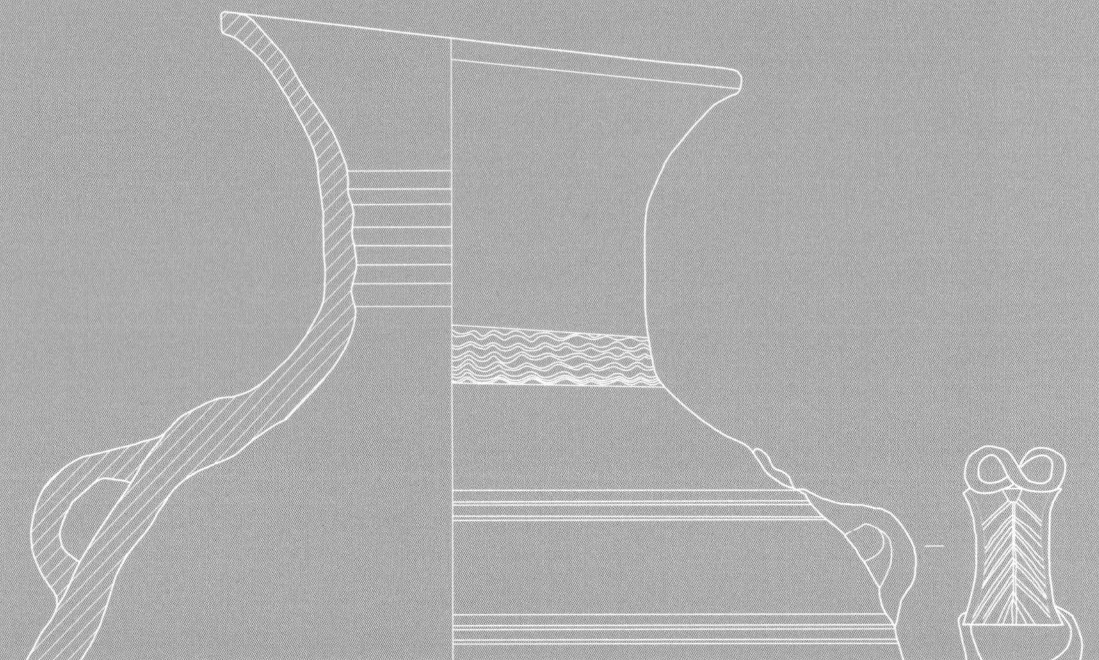
0 1厘米

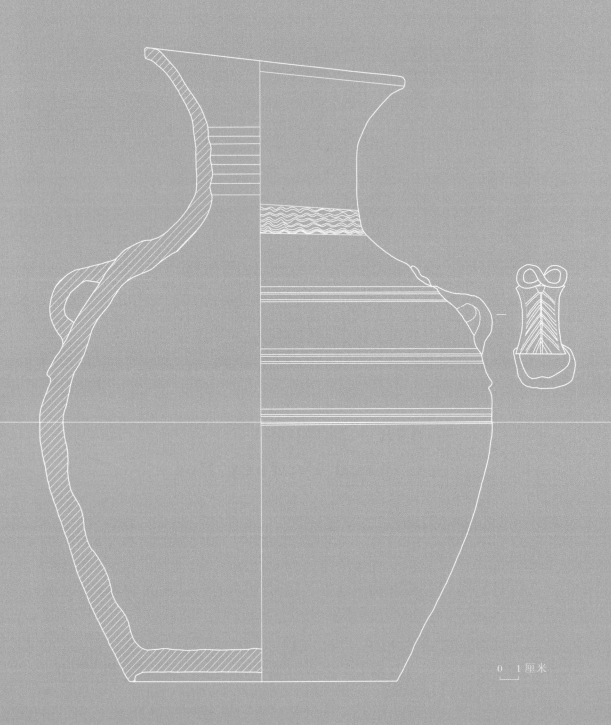

059 釉陶壶
Glazed Pottery Pot

汉

螺蛳墩遗址出土（M4：5）

口径 14.2 厘米、底径 15.2 厘米、高 34.7 厘米

夹砂硬陶质。喇叭口，圆唇，束颈，溜肩，鼓腹，下腹斜收，隐圈足。口沿倾斜，肩部贴饰一对叶脉纹桥形耳，另有两组弦纹，上腹有一组凹凸弦纹，下腹可见多组轮制凹凸弦纹，上腹至口沿部施青釉，下腹及底足无釉。

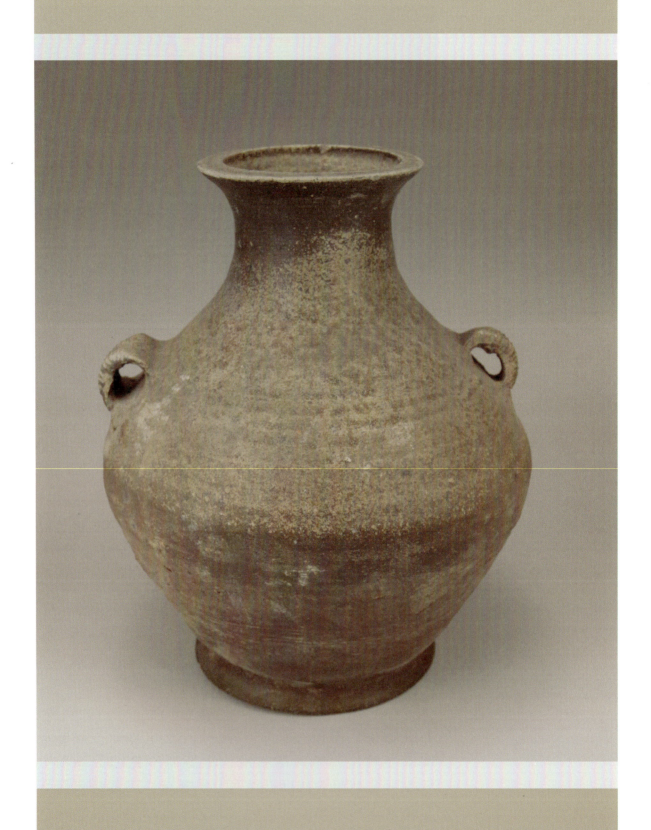

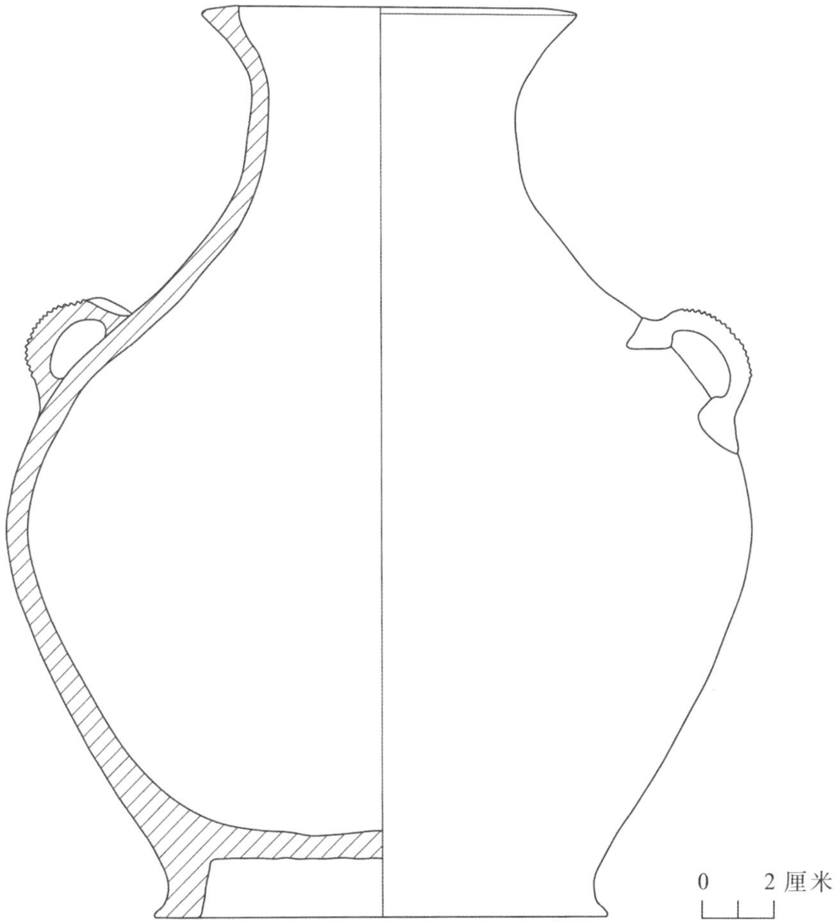

060 釉陶壶

Glazed Pottery Pot

汉

月城遗址采集

口径 7.8 厘米、底径 12.6 厘米、最大腹径 20.8 厘米、高 24. 8 厘米

夹砂硬陶质。敛口，平沿，尖唇，束颈，溜肩，鼓腹。下腹斜收，喇叭形圈足，足端宽平。肩部贴饰一对叶脉纹桥形耳，肩部可见轮制凹凸弦纹，上腹至口沿部施青釉，下腹及底足无釉。

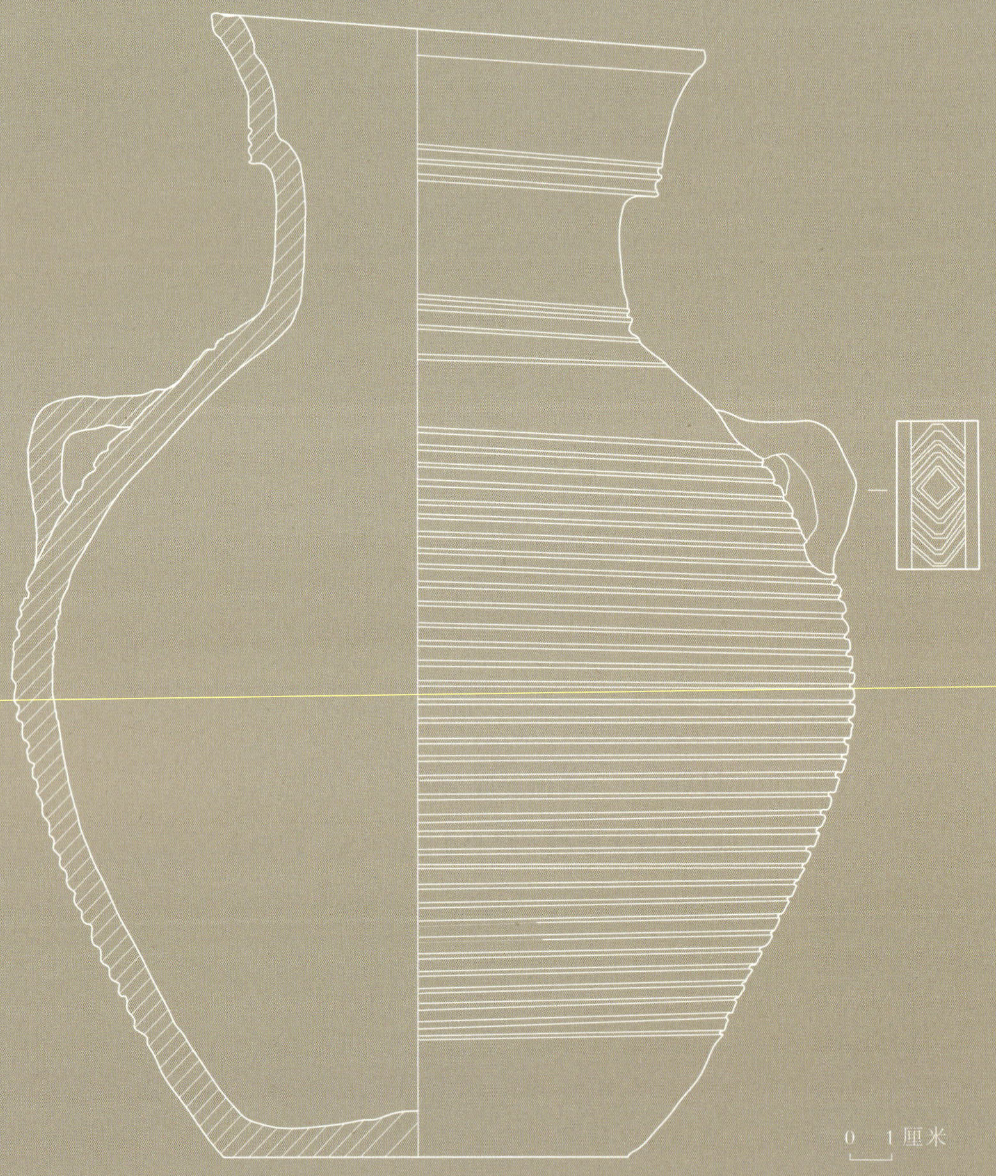
0 1厘米

061 釉陶壶
Glazed Pottery Pot

汉
螺蛳墩遗址出土（M8：9）
内口径 10.7 厘米、底径 10 厘米、最大腹径 21.2 厘米、高 27.2 厘米

夹砂硬陶质。盘口，平沿内凹，圆厚唇，束直颈，溜肩，鼓腹，下腹斜收，平底内凹。口下部有一组凹凸弦纹，颈下部有一组凸弦纹，肩部贴饰一对叶脉纹桥形耳，肩腹部通体饰凹凸弦纹。通体施青釉，脱釉严重。

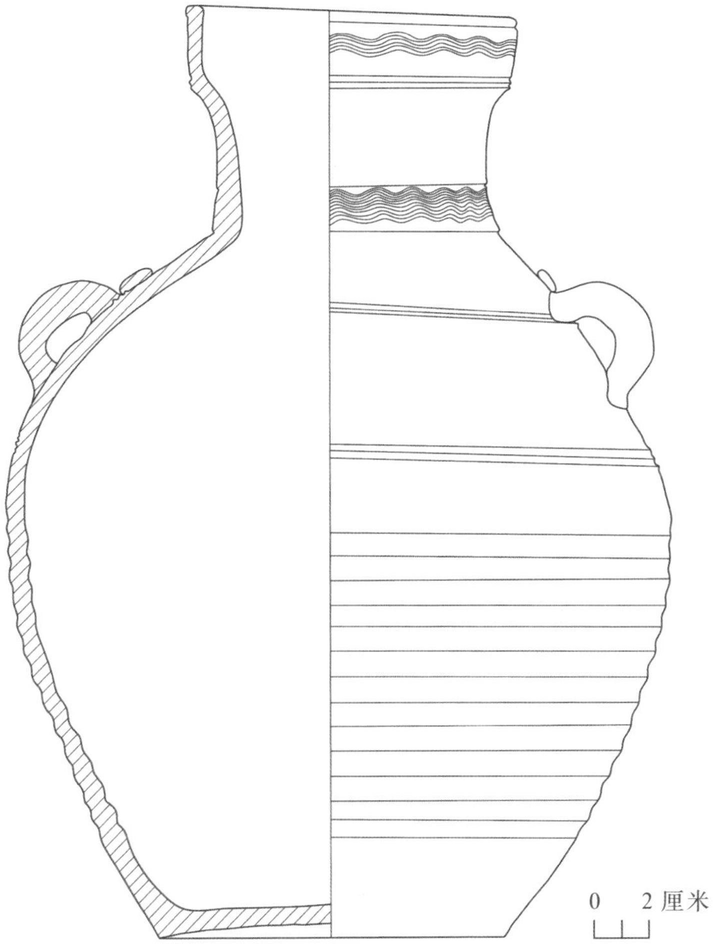

062 釉陶壶

Glazed Pottery Pot

汉

月城遗址采集

口径 11 厘米、底径 12 厘米、最大腹径 24 厘米、高 32.5 厘米

夹砂硬陶质。盘口，圆唇，束直颈，溜肩，鼓腹，下腹斜收，小底内凹。近口沿处和颈下部均装饰一组水波纹，肩部饰一对叶脉纹桥形耳，两组凹凸弦纹，腹部可见多条凹凸粗线纹。肩部及以上施青釉，脱釉严重，腹部及以下无釉。

0 2厘米

063　釉陶壶
Glazed Pottery Pot

汉

螺蛳墩遗址出土（M8：8）

口径 14 厘米、底径 15.2 厘米、最大腹径 28.8 厘米、高 35.2 厘米

夹砂硬陶质。盘口，圆唇，束颈，溜肩，鼓腹，喇叭形圈足。口沿外壁有两组凹凸弦纹，肩部贴塑一对如意头桥形耳，肩腹部有多条凹凸弦纹。通体施青釉，脱釉严重。

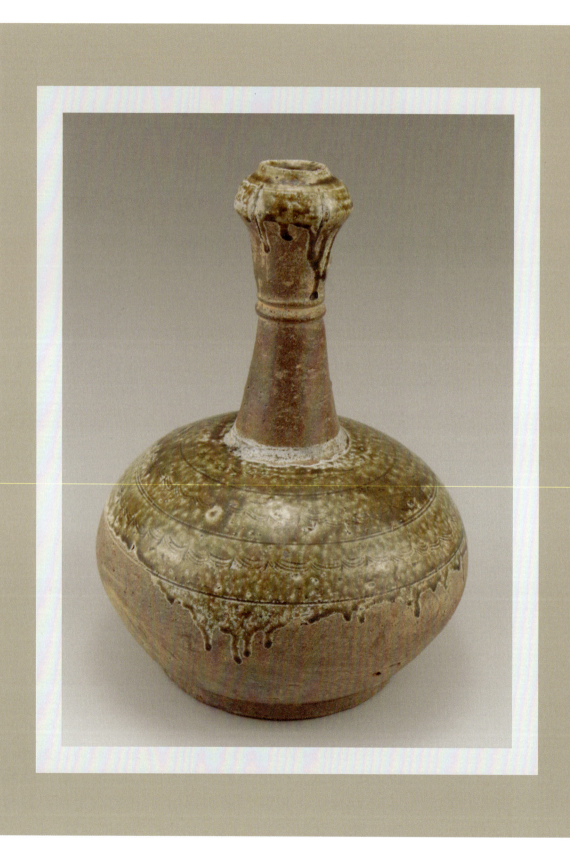

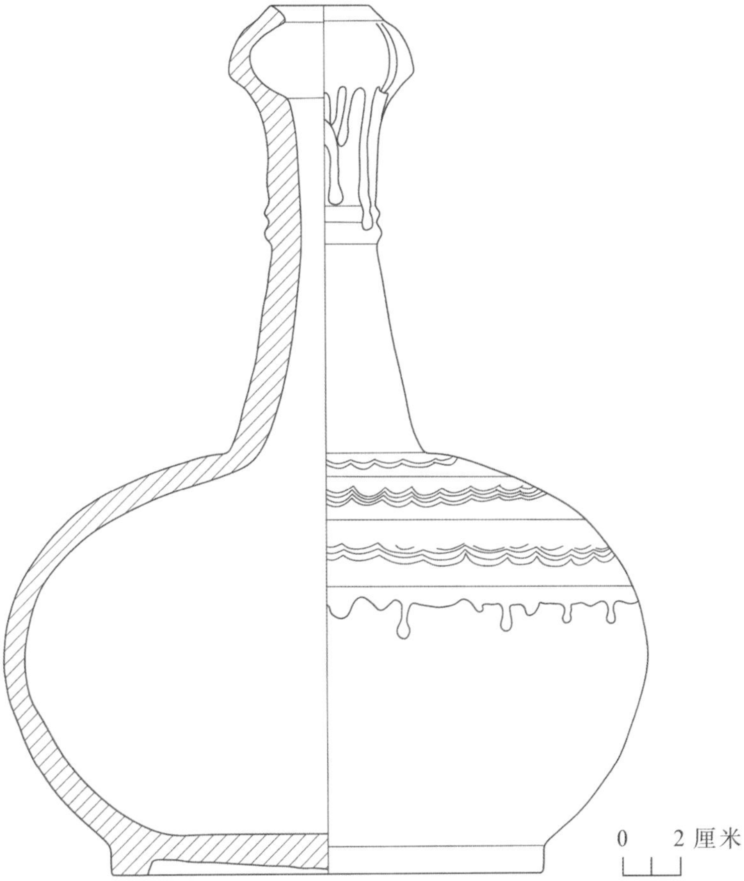

064 釉陶壶
Glazed Pottery Pot

汉

征集

内口径3.2厘米、底径14.7厘米、最大腹径22厘米、高28.5厘米

夹砂硬陶质。小敞口，长束颈，溜肩，扁鼓腹，大圈足。颈上部有五条竖向凹槽，中部饰一周凸棱纹，肩部饰三组弦纹间隔的水波纹。口部和肩部施青釉，局部流釉。

065　陶麟趾金

Pottery Hoof-Shaped Coin

汉

月城遗址采集

直径 8.2 厘米、高 2.8 厘米

夹砂硬陶质。似馒头形，顶面弧凸，饰星云纹，底面近平，略有凹凸。

066 陶井圈

Pottery Circel of Well

汉

月城遗址采集

直径 68 厘米、高 36.5 厘米、壁厚 3.2 厘米

夹砂灰陶质。圆形，直筒状，上下两端面及外壁满饰绳纹。

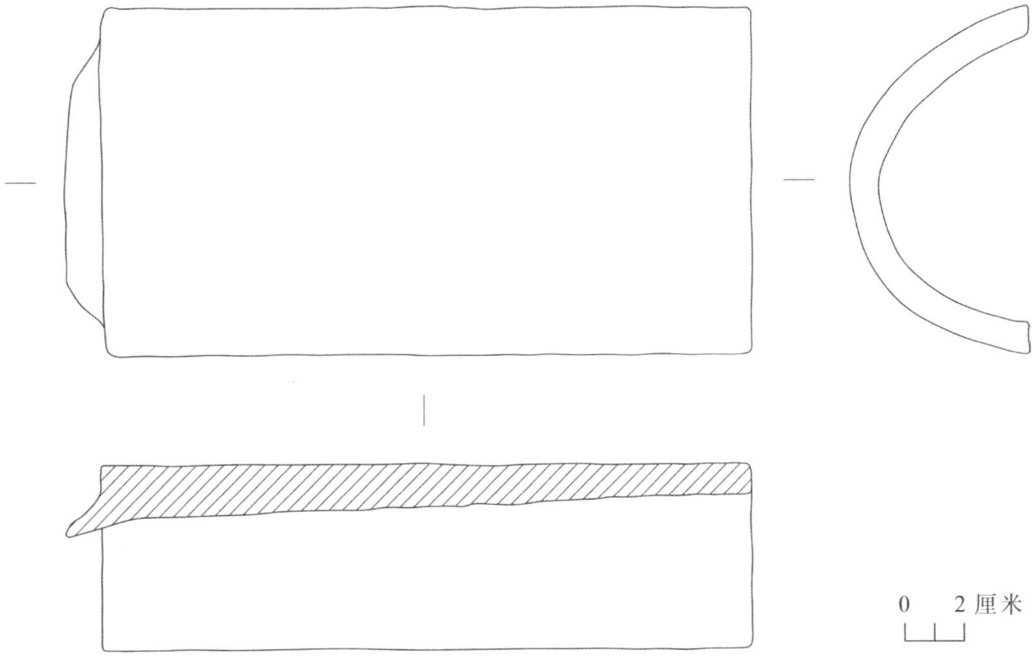

067 陶筒瓦

Pottery Pantile

汉

月城遗址采集

长 45.5 厘米、宽 22.5 厘米、拱高 12 厘米、壁厚 2.5 厘米

夹砂灰陶质。器身呈半圆形，一端平直，一端略瘦细，似台阶状。器形宽大，壁面厚重。

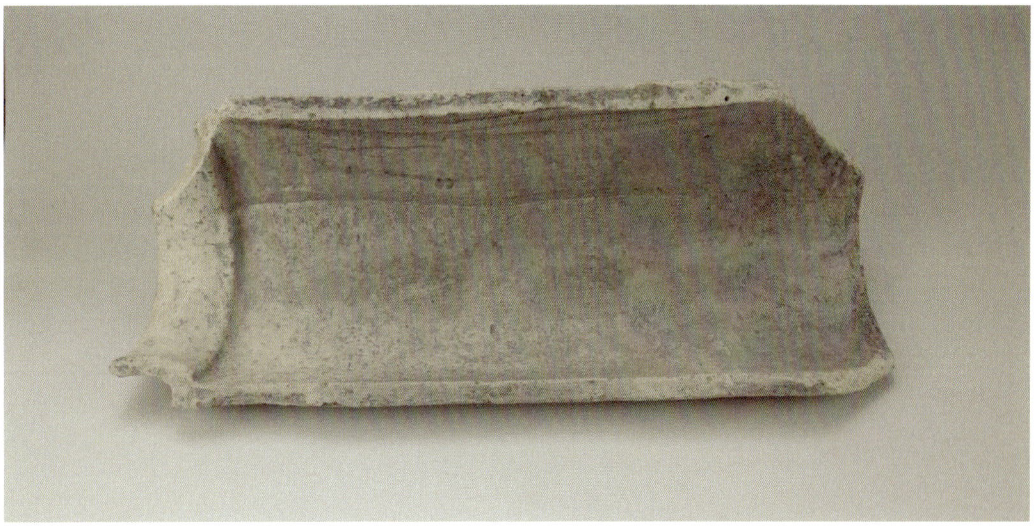

068　陶筒瓦
Pottery Pantile

汉

月城遗址采集

长 37.2 厘米、厚 1 厘米，宽 14.3 厘米、拱高 7.6 厘米

夹砂灰陶质。器身呈半圆形，一端平直，一端略瘦细，似台阶状。器形瘦长，壁面厚薄。

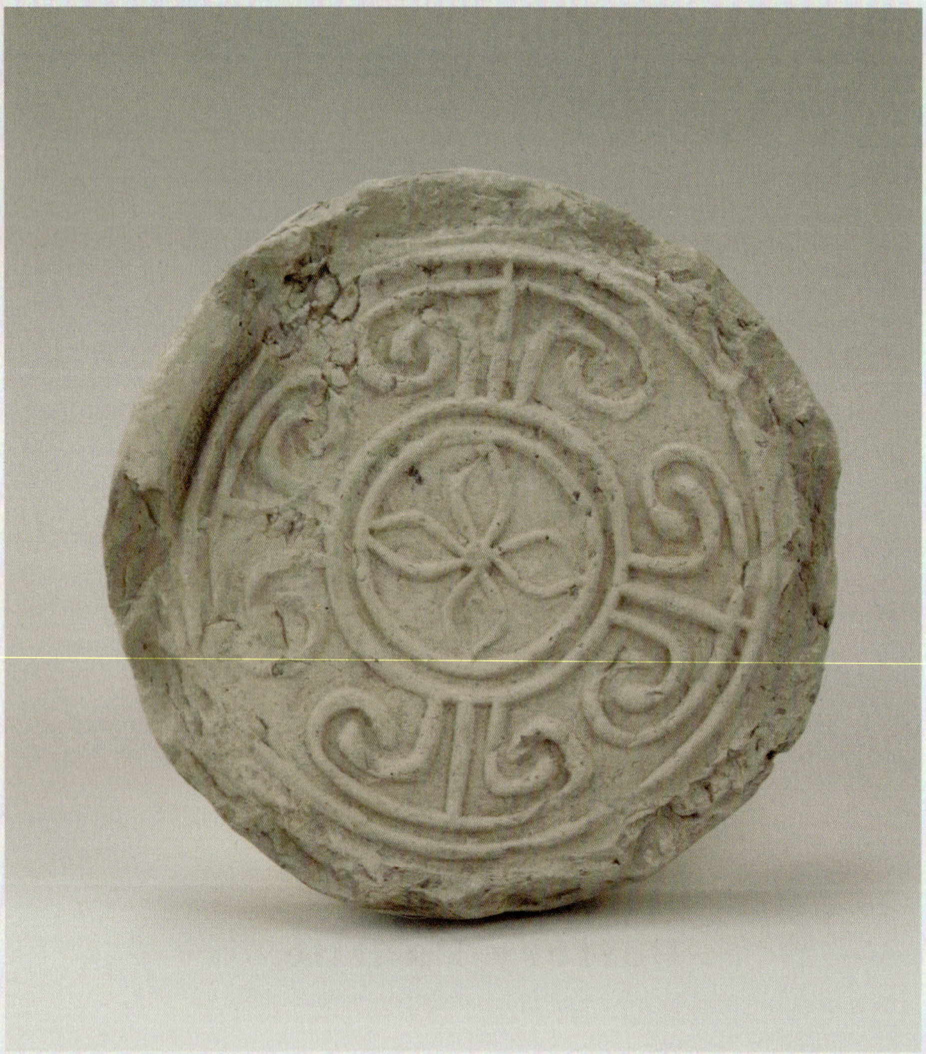

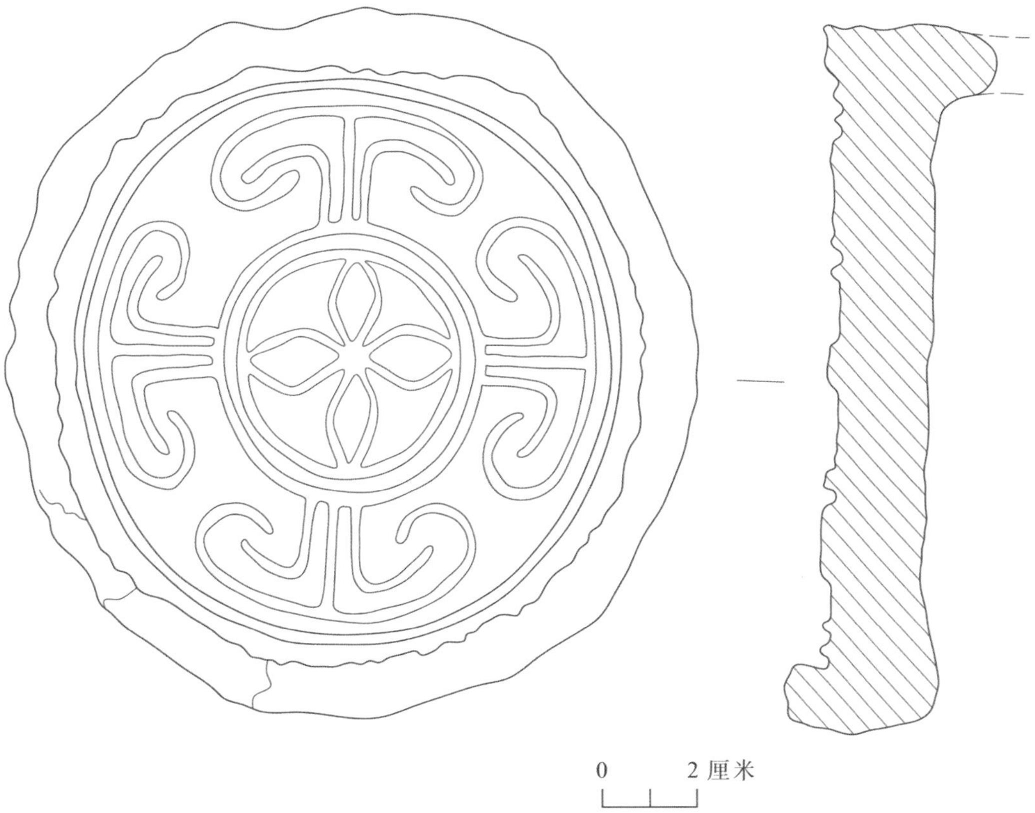

069　陶瓦当
Pottery Eaves Tile

汉

月城遗址采集

直径 14 厘米、壁厚 2 厘米

夹砂灰陶质。圆饼形，身部残缺。端面外表有一周凸棱，大部残缺。端面外表另凸印一周弦纹和四组卷云纹，中心部位凸印双弦纹和四叶草纹。

070 陶瓦当
Pottery Eaves Tile

汉

月城遗址采集

直径 16 厘米、厚 2.7 厘米

夹砂灰陶质。圆饼形，身部残缺。外表面有一周凸棱，微残。端面外表四周另凸印四组卷云纹，中心部位凸印菱形方格纹。

071 陶瓦当
Pottery Eaves Tile

汉

月城遗址采集

直径 15 厘米、壁厚 2.3 厘米

夹砂灰陶质。端面呈圆饼形，身部呈半圆筒状。端面外表有一周凸棱，端面外围另凸印四组卷云纹，中心部位凸印方格纹。瓦身外表通体印绳纹。

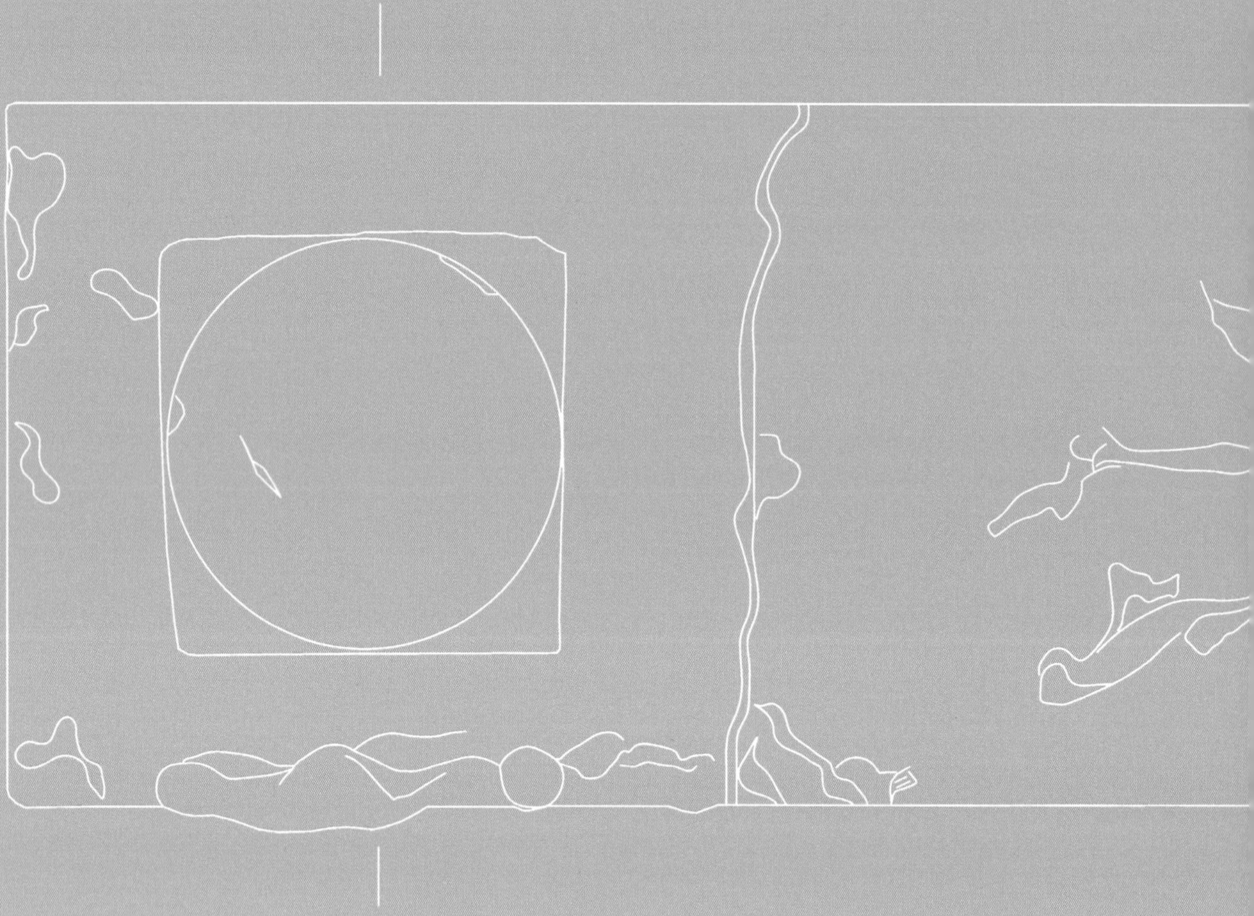

072　石黛板
Stone Daiban

汉

螺蛳墩遗址出土（M5：10）

长 12.5 厘米、宽 5 厘米、通高 1.8 厘米

石质。由研石和研板组成。研石上圆下方。研板呈长方形，板状。

0
1 厘米

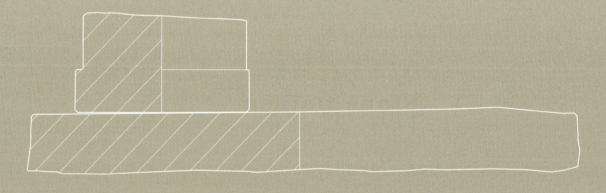

073　石黛板

Stone Daiban

汉

螺蛳墩遗址出土（M8：1）

长 9.5 厘米、宽 5 厘米、通高 2.7 厘米

石质。由研石和研板组成。研石上圆下方。研板呈长方形，板状。

0
1厘米

074　铜镜

Bronze Mirror

汉

螺蛳墩遗址出土（M4：8）

直径 8.6 厘米、最厚 0.95 厘米

铜质。连弧铭文镜，圆形。正面光素，微弧起，背面中心有圆钮，带穿孔。背面内区主体纹饰由连弧纹、斜线纹和铭文带组成，外区素宽。

0
2 厘米

075　铜镜
Bronze Mirror

汉

螺蛳墩遗址出土（M4：16）

直径 10.2 厘米、最厚 0.6 厘米

铜质。四乳四螭镜，圆形。正面光素，微弧起，背面中心有圆钮，带穿孔。背面内区主体纹饰为四乳钉相间的极为简化的四螭（四虺）和两周斜线纹，外区素宽。

0 1厘米

076　铜镜
Bronze Mirror

汉
螺蛳墩遗址出土（M5：1）
直径 13 厘米、最厚 1.3 厘米

铜质。连弧铭文镜，圆形。正面光素，微弧起，背面中心有圆钮，带穿孔。背面内区主体纹饰由乳钉纹、连弧纹、斜线纹和铭文带组成，外区素宽。

0
2 厘米

077　铜镜

Bronze Mirror

汉

螺蛳墩遗址出土（M5：9）

直径 9.4 厘米、厚 0.7 厘米

铜质。连弧铭文镜，圆形。正面光素，微弧起，背面中心有圆钮，带穿孔。背面内区主体纹饰自内向外依次由内向八连弧纹，斜线纹，铭文带和斜线纹组成，铭文模糊，似“昭明镜”，外区较素宽。

0
2 厘米

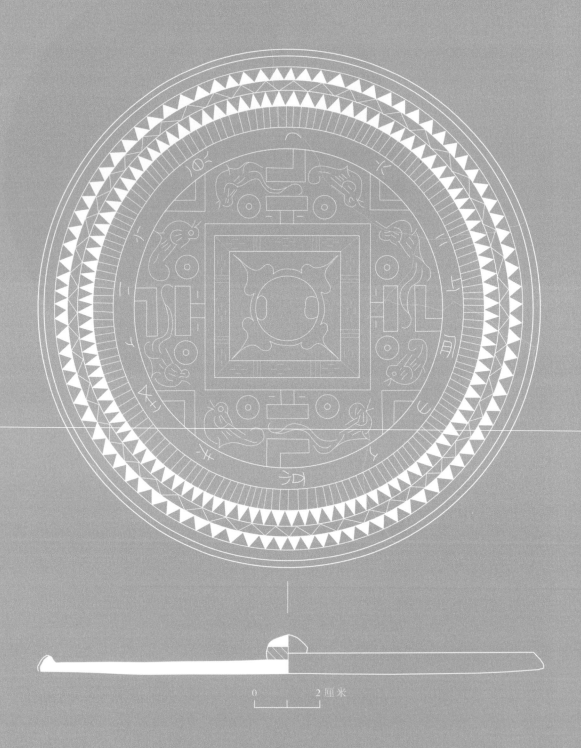

078　铜镜
Bronze Mirror

汉

螺蛳墩遗址出土（M8：3）

直径 15.4 厘米、最厚 1.05 厘米

铜质。博局八乳八鸟镜，圆形。正面光素，平整，背面中心有圆钮，中空。背面内区主体纹饰由博局纹、八乳八鸟纹、铭文带和一周射线纹组成，铭文模糊不明，外区自内向外由一周锯齿纹、一周折线纹和一周锯齿纹组成。外缘部呈三角凸棱形。

0
2厘米

079　铜镜
Bronze Mirror

汉
螺蛳墩遗址出土（M8：2）
直径 13.1 厘米、最厚 1.2 厘米

铜质。博局八乳八鸟镜，圆形。正面光素，平整，背面中心有圆钮，中空。背面内区主体纹饰由博局纹、八乳八鸟纹、铭文带和一周射线纹组成，铭文模糊不明，外区自内向外由一周锯齿纹、一周折线纹和一周锯齿纹组成。外缘部呈凸棱形。

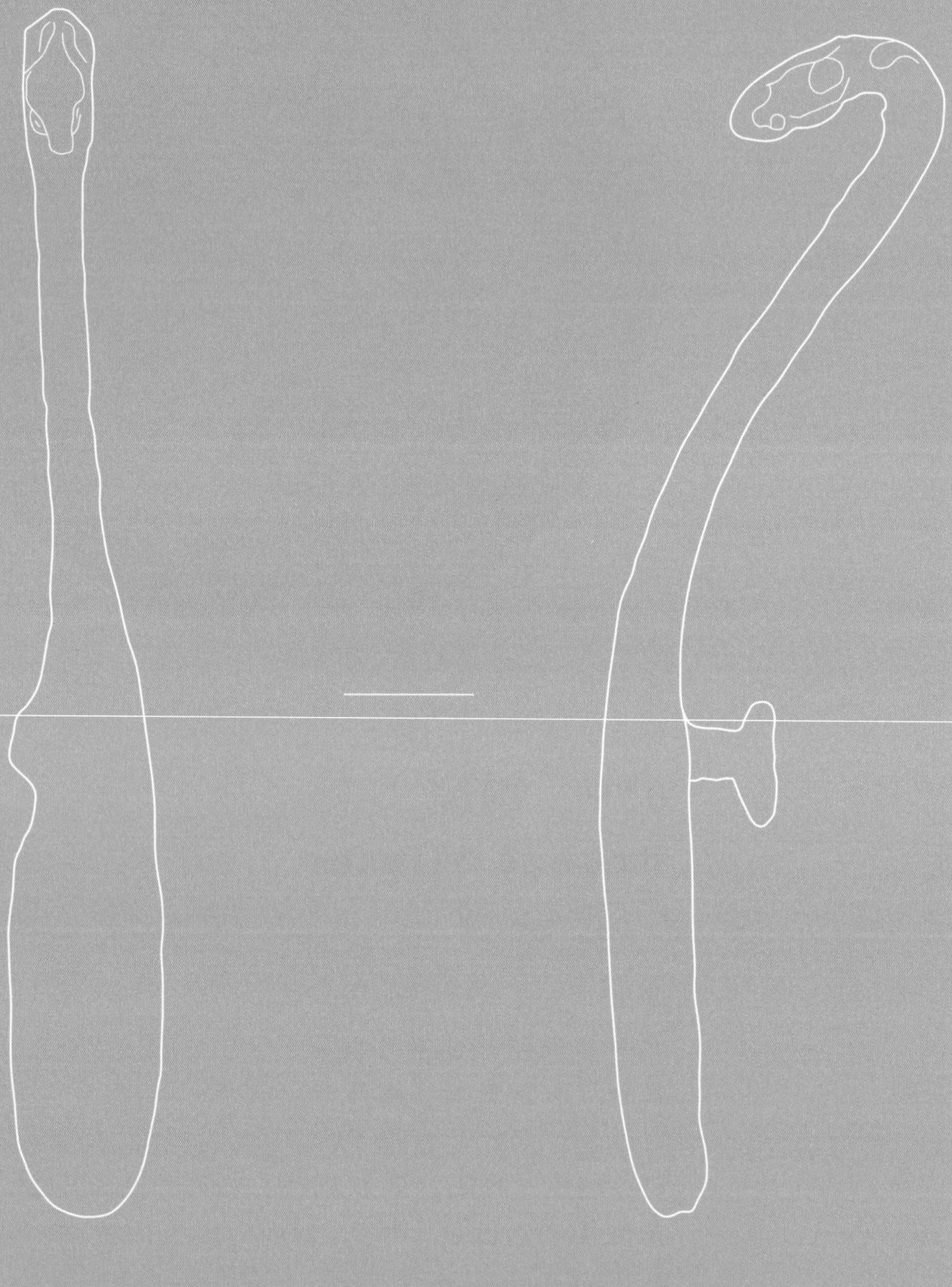

0
2 厘米

080　铜带钩

Bronze Belt Hook

汉

螺蛳墩遗址出土（M5：6）

长 11 厘米、最宽 1.4 厘米

铜质。器身呈琵琶形，兽头形钩首上扬，钩身腹部背面有一铆钉钮。

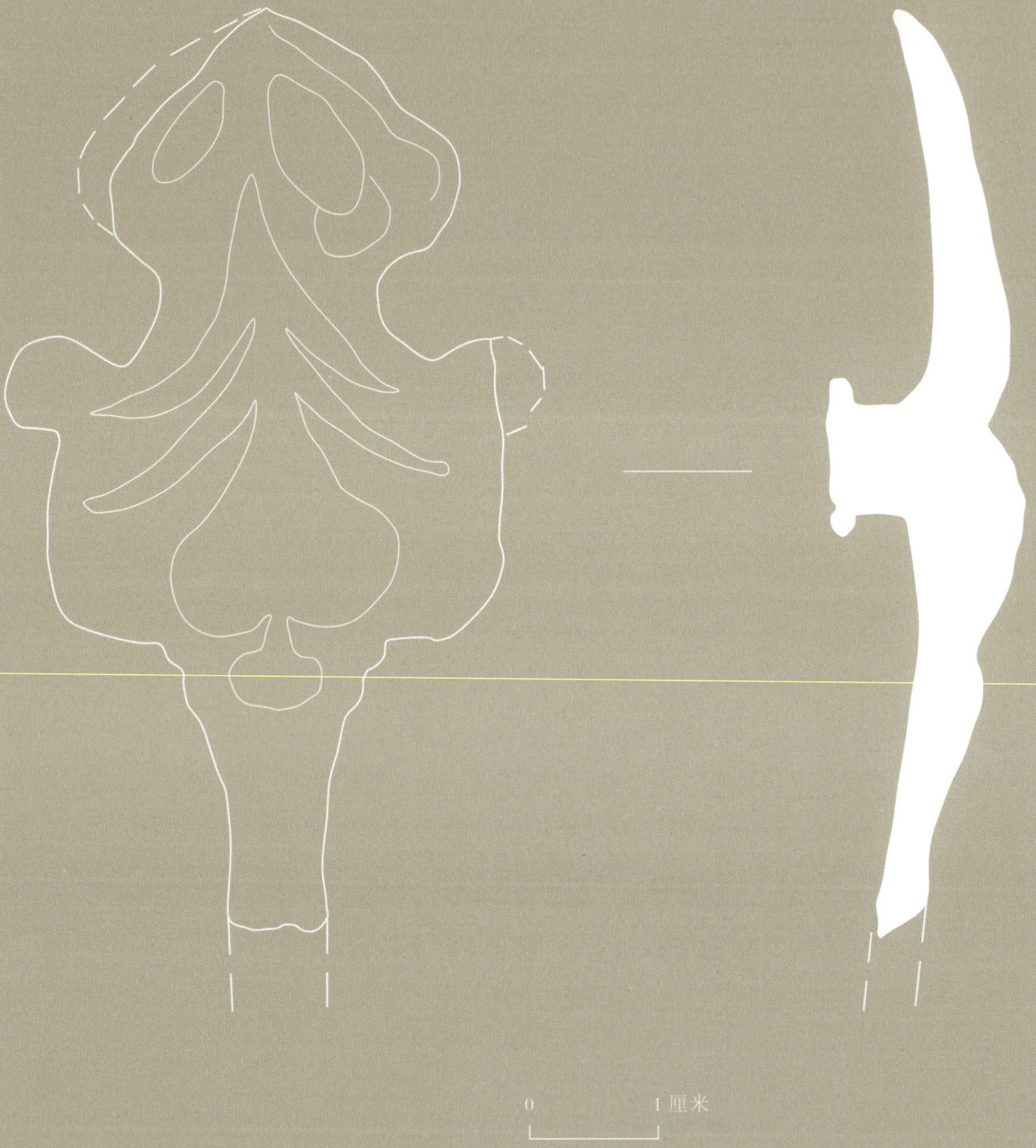
0
1厘米

081 铜带钩
Bronze Belt Hook

汉
螺蛳墩遗址出（M4：12）
残长 7 厘米、最宽 4.2 厘米

铜质。器身呈鸟形，首宽尾窄，器身弯曲，似“S”形。首部似鸟展翅状，正面纹饰模糊，背面有凸起圆钮，尾部细长，正面有凸起圆钮，背面光素。

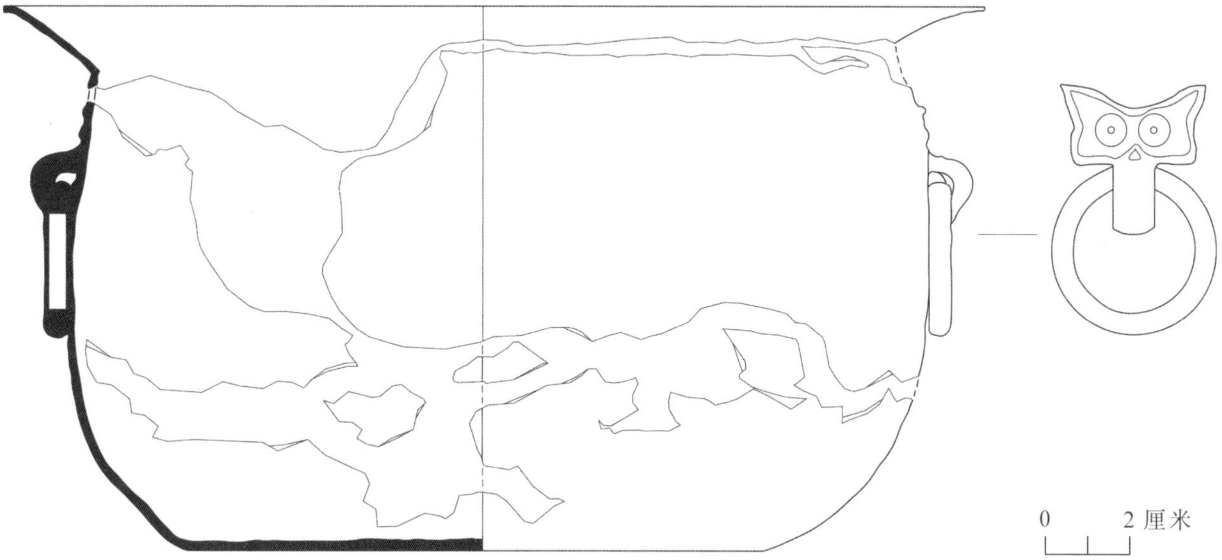

082 铜釜
Bronze Cauldron

汉

螺蛳墩遗址（M4：7）

口径 22.9 厘米、底径 13.8 厘米、最大腹径 20.2 厘米、高 12.4 厘米

铜质。喇叭口，尖唇、外折沿，深弧腹，平底。上腹近口部微束，腹部有一对铺首衔环耳，另有凹凸弦纹。通体锈蚀碎裂，残损严重。

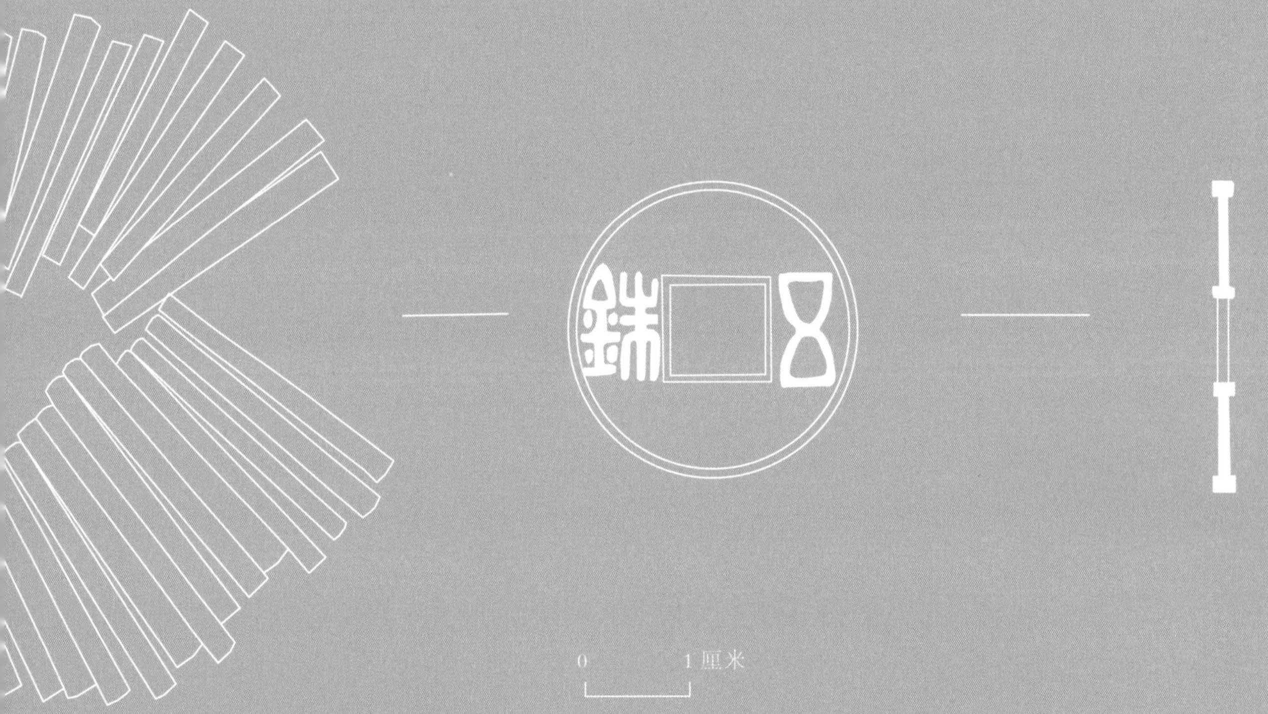

083　五铢铜钱
“Wuzhu” Coins

汉

螺蛳墩遗址出土（M4：11）

单体直径 2.5 厘米、厚 0.15 厘米

铜质。一串，锈蚀严重，145± 枚。单体圆形方孔，正面自右向左篆书“五铢”，背面光素。

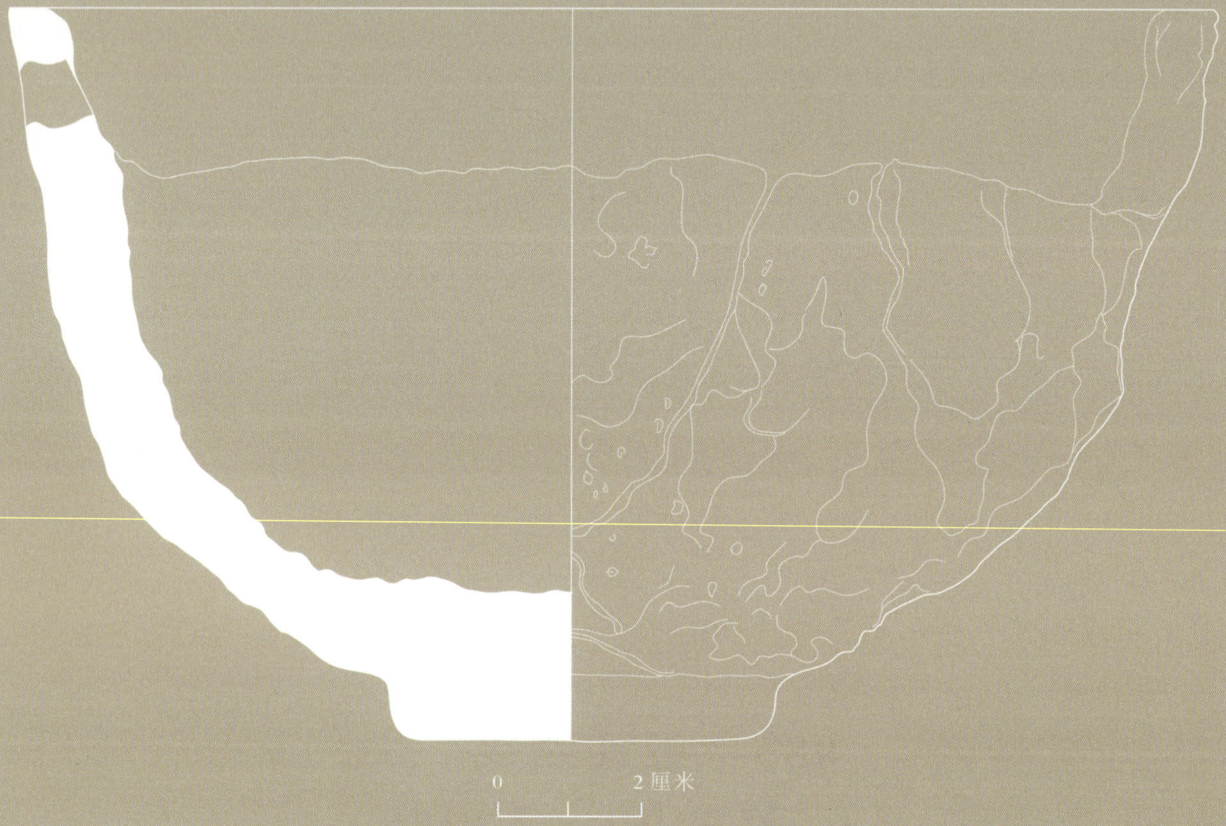
0
2 厘米

084 铁釜

Iron Cauldron

汉

螺蛳墩遗址出土（M16：15）

口径 18 厘米、高 9.8 厘米

铁质。敞直口，斜弧腹，圈足底。口沿处附一对立耳，中空。通体锈蚀严重。

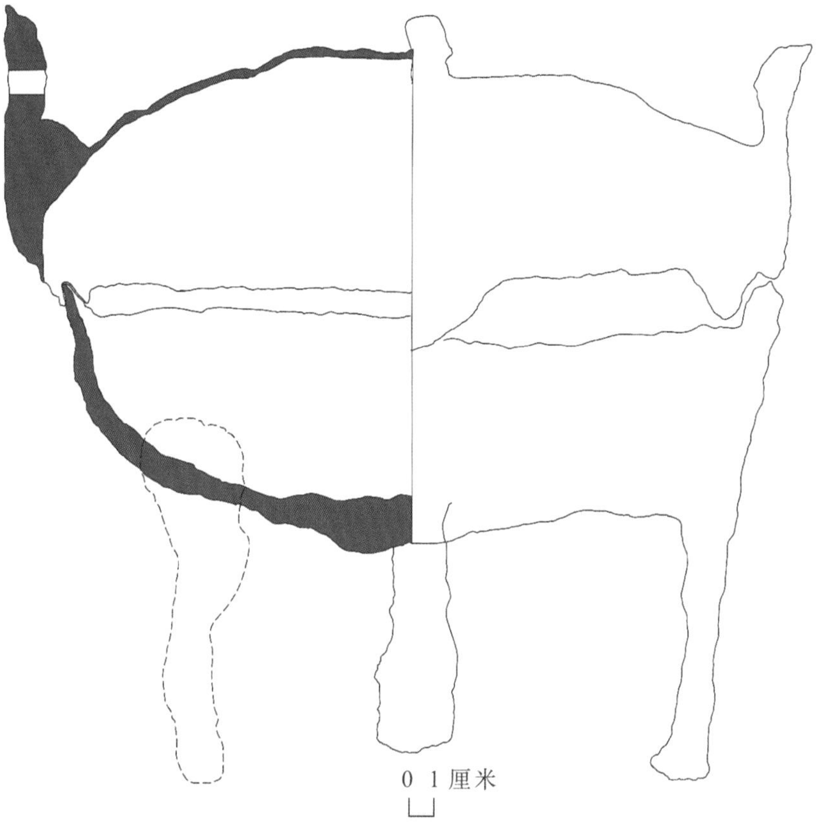

085 铁鼎
Iron Tripod Caldron

汉

螺蛳墩遗址出土（M16：5）

最大径 27.4 厘米、通高 30.5 厘米

铁质。由鼎盖和鼎身组成。鼎盖呈帽形，子口，微内敛，顶部中心有一凸钮，两侧有一对立耳，中空，微外撇。鼎身呈口锅形，母口，微外撇，圜底，三高足。通体锈蚀碎裂严重。

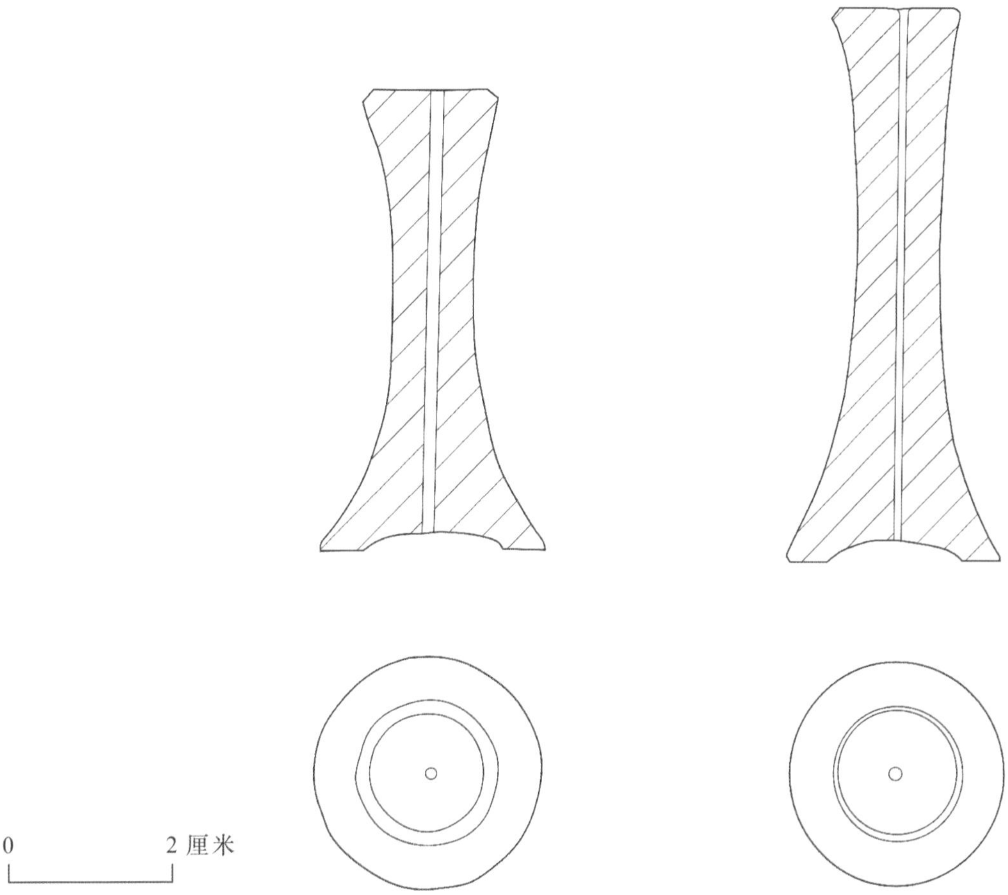

086 琉璃耳珰
Glass Earplug（Erdang）

汉
螺蛳墩遗址出土（M8：4、M8：5）
最大直径 1.35 厘米、高 2.7 厘米

琉璃质。色蓝，喇叭形，柱状，束腰，中心有贯穿细孔。两端面呈圆形，一端略大，内凹，一端略小，较平整。

087　青砖
Brick

六朝
月城遗址采集
长 28.5 厘米、宽 10—11.5 厘米、厚 4 厘米

泥质灰陶质。砖身近似长方体形，微残。横端面有刻印莲花纹。

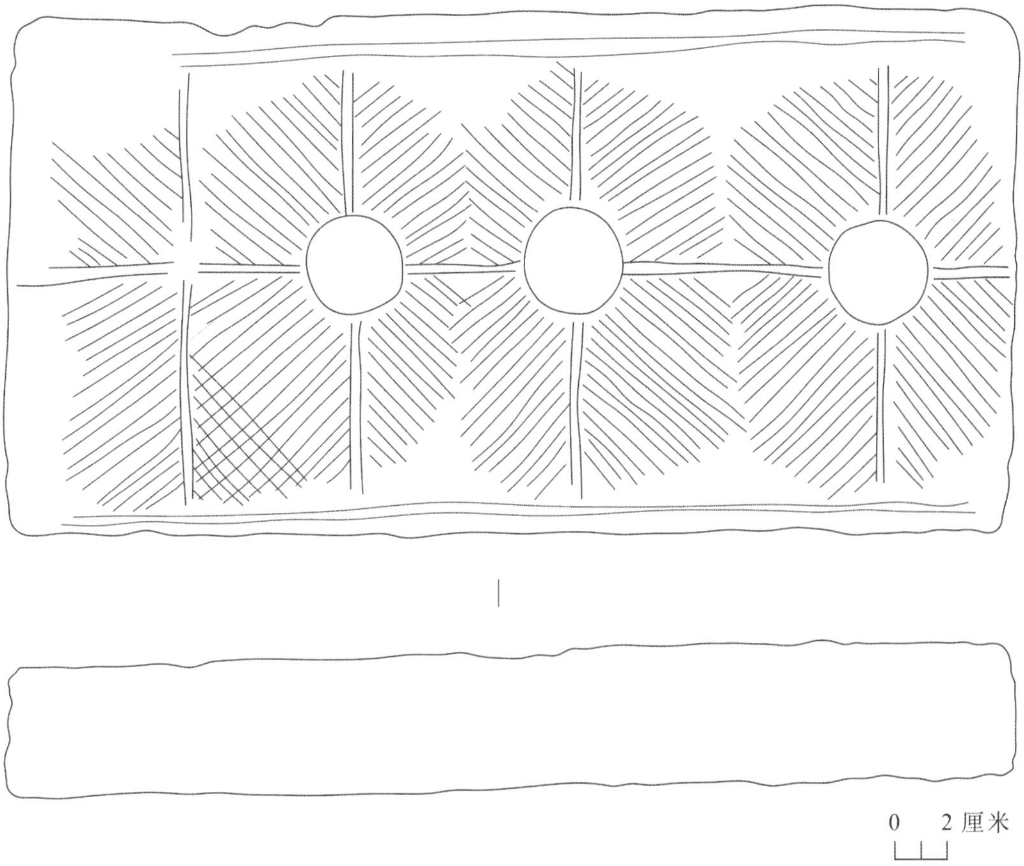

088　青砖

Brick

六朝

豨巷遗址采集

长 38.2 厘米、宽 19 厘米、厚 4.6 厘米

泥质灰陶质。砖身呈长方体形。砖面凸印斜线纹和太阳花纹。砖体宽大厚重，胎色泛红。

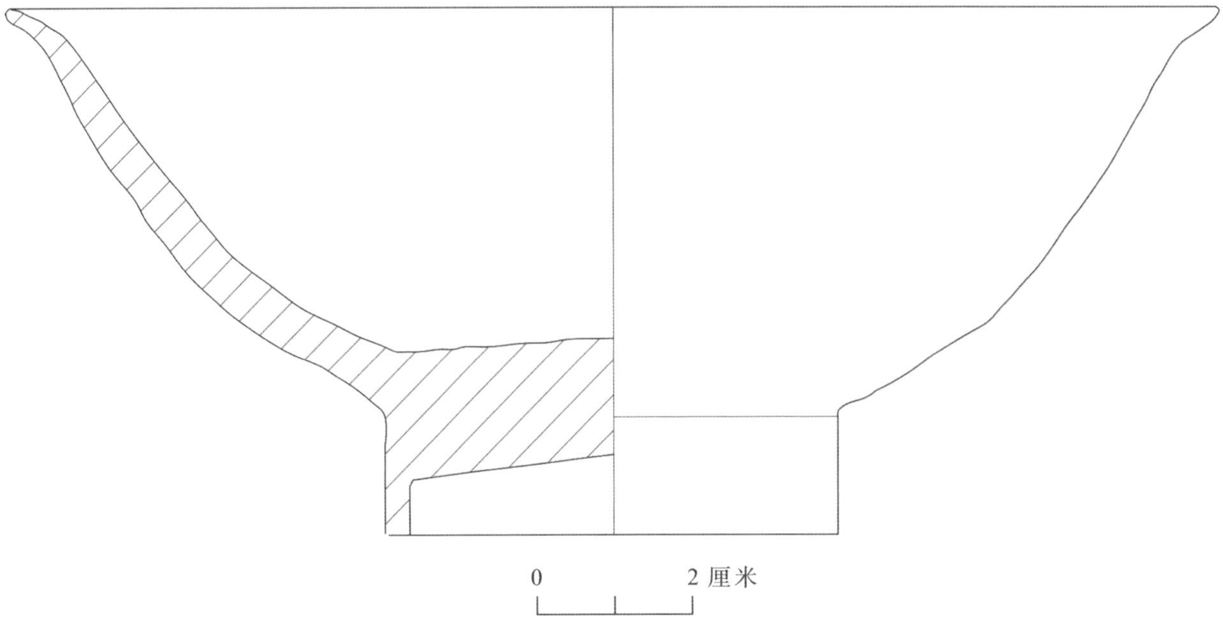

089 青瓷碗
Celadon Bowl

唐

螺蛳墩遗址出土（M1：1）

口径 15.8 厘米、底径 5.8 厘米、高 6.7 厘米

青瓷质。敞侈口，圆唇，斜弧腹，圈足。圈足略高，素面。通体施青釉，足部无釉。

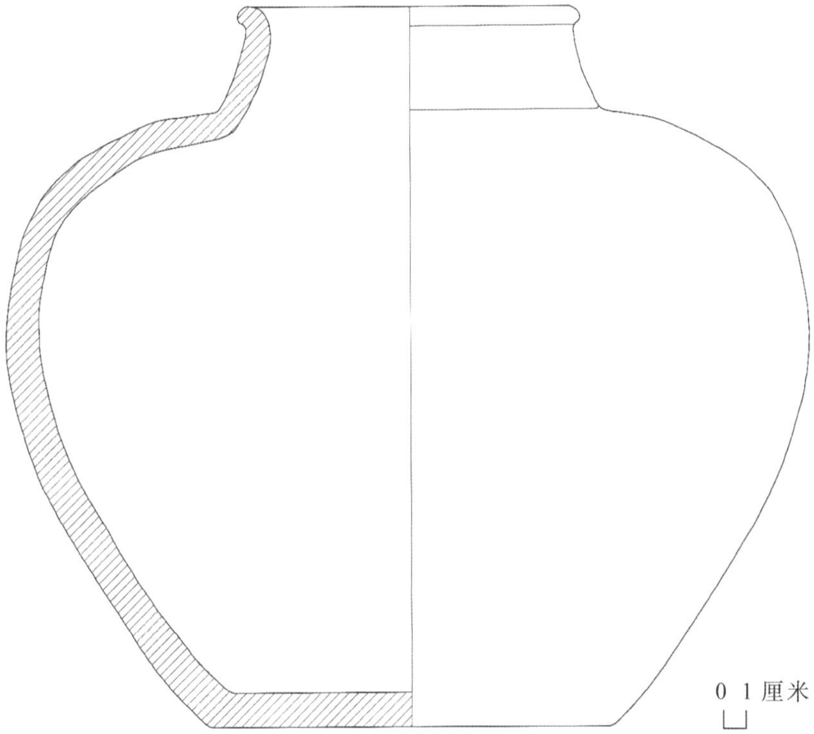

090　釉陶罐
Glazed Pottery Jar

唐

螺蛳墩遗址出土（M3：2）

口径 13.6 厘米、底径 17.4 厘米、高 29.8 厘米

釉陶质。小口，微侈，圆厚唇，短颈，丰肩，圆鼓腹，平底。外壁口部、颈部和上腹部施酱褐釉，下腹及底部无釉。施釉厚薄不均，釉色暗淡，胎质较硬。

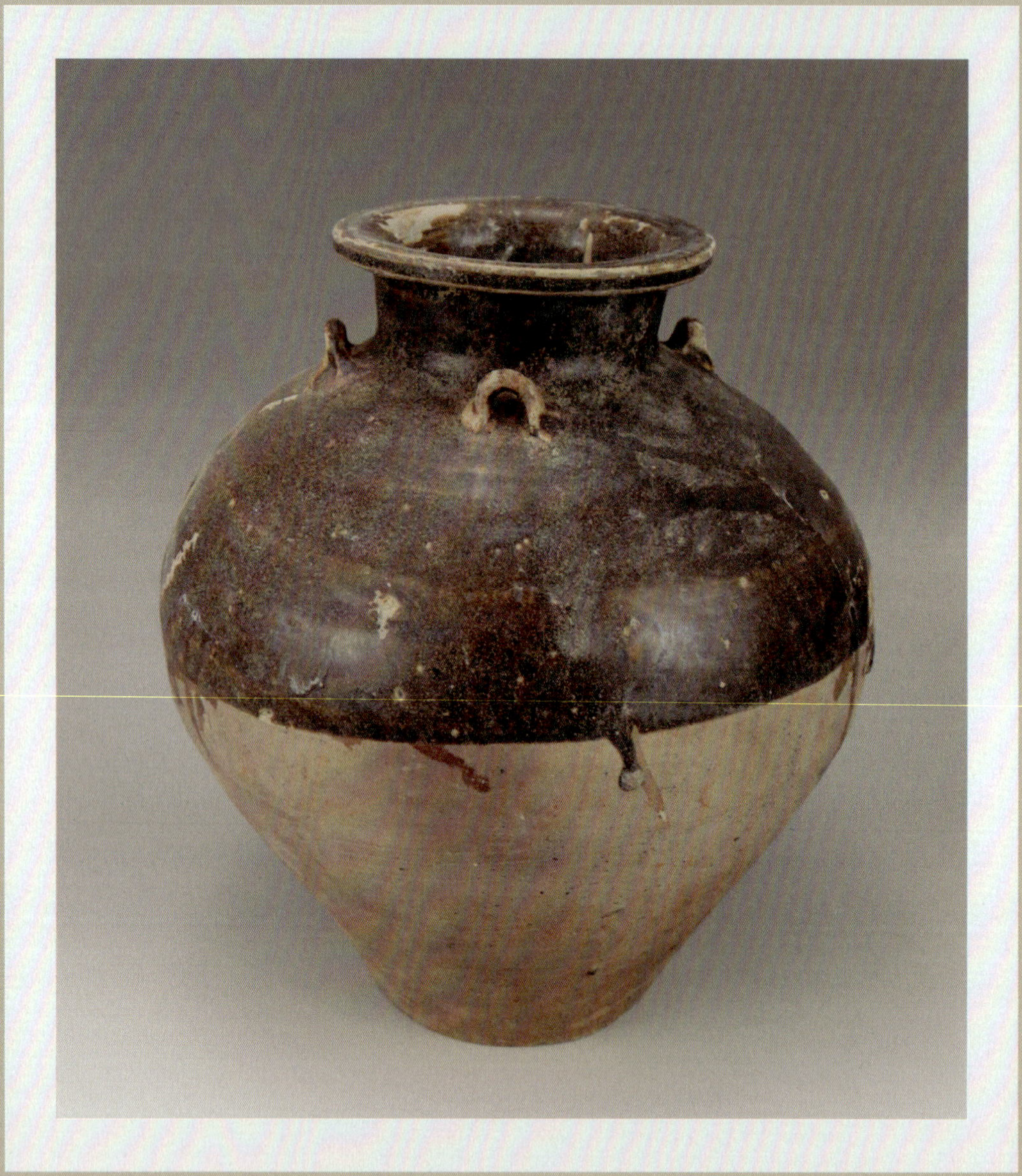

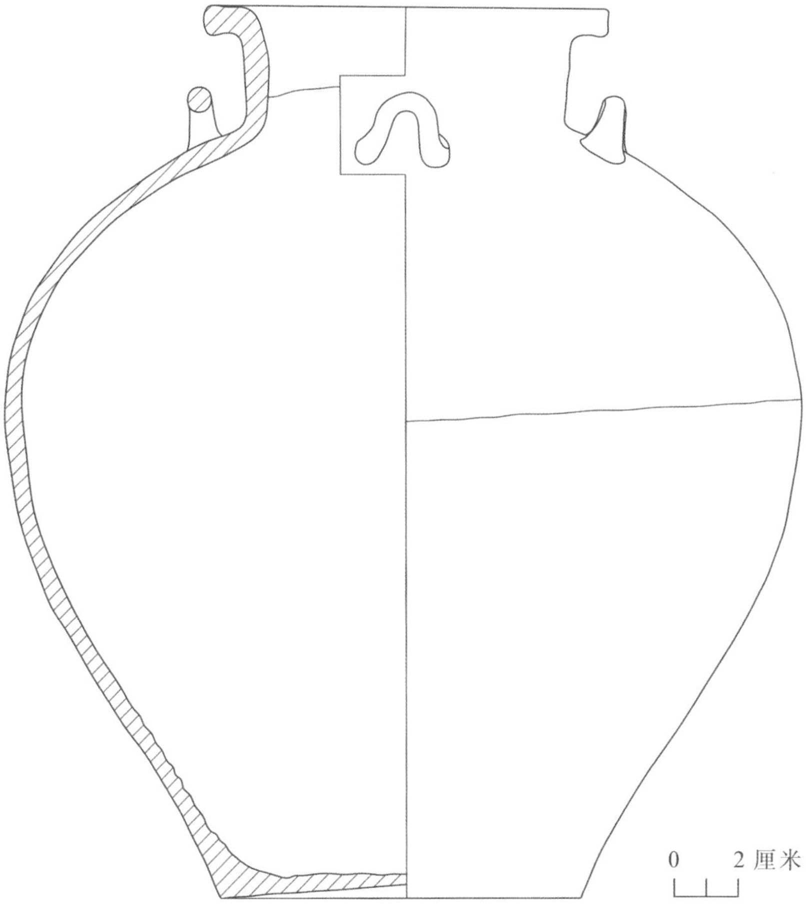

091　釉陶罐

Glazed Pottery Jar

唐

月城遗址出土

口径 9.8 厘米、底径 11.4 厘米、最大腹径 25 厘米、高 27 厘米

釉陶质。侈口，平面外折，方唇，短束颈，溜肩，鼓腹，下腹斜收，小平底，略内凹。肩部贴饰两对桥形耳，器身上部满施酱褐釉，下腹及底部无釉，胎质较硬。

092　陶碾轮
Pottery Runner Wheel

唐宋
月城遗址采集
复原直径 11 厘米、厚 2.4 厘米

夹砂灰陶质。圆饼形，残缺一半。中部厚，四周略薄，中心有圆形穿孔，磨制光滑。

093　陶碾轮
Pottery Runner Wheel

唐宋
月城遗址采集
复原直径 10.5 厘米、厚 2.3 厘米

夹砂红陶质。圆饼形，残缺一半。中部厚，四周略薄，中心有圆形穿孔，磨制光滑。

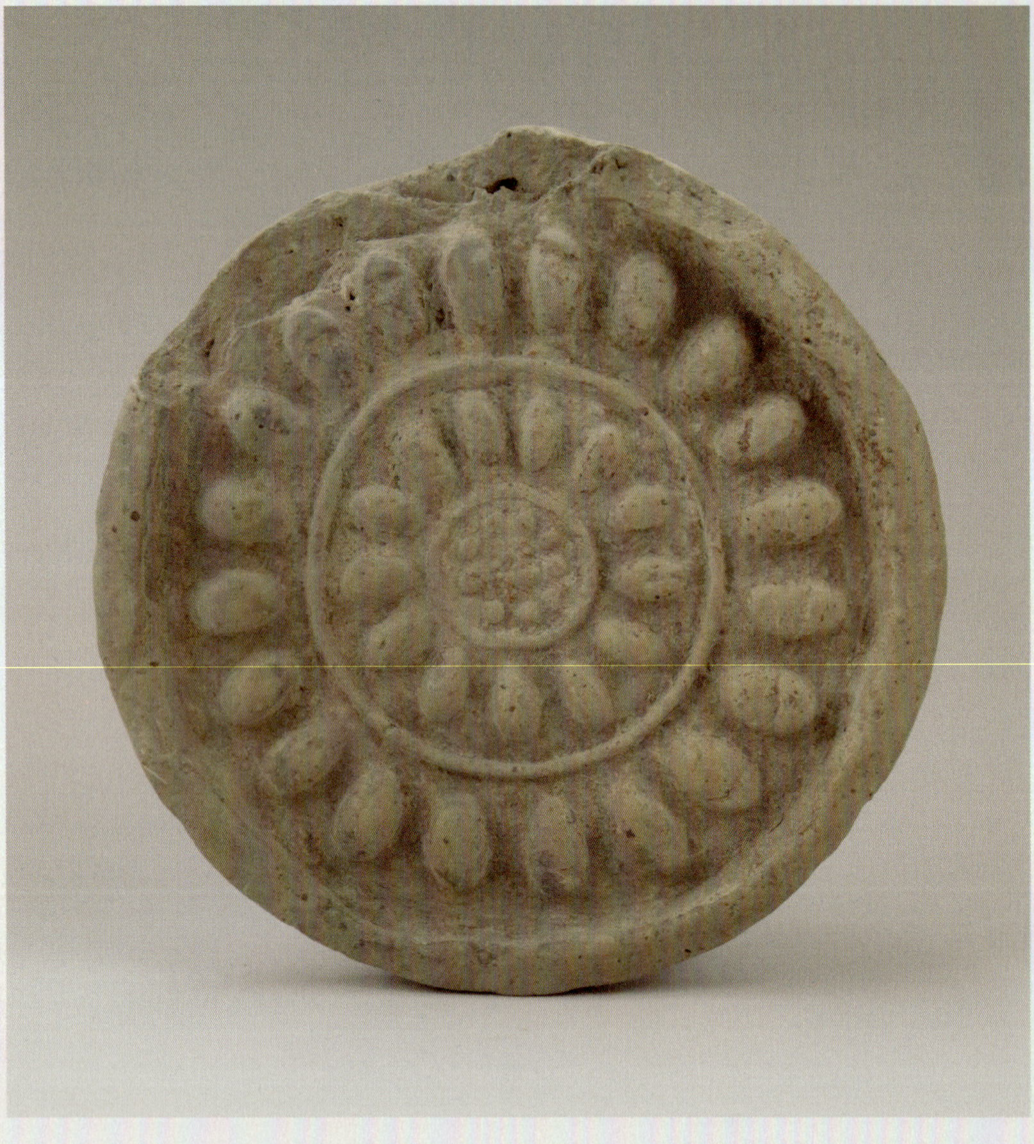

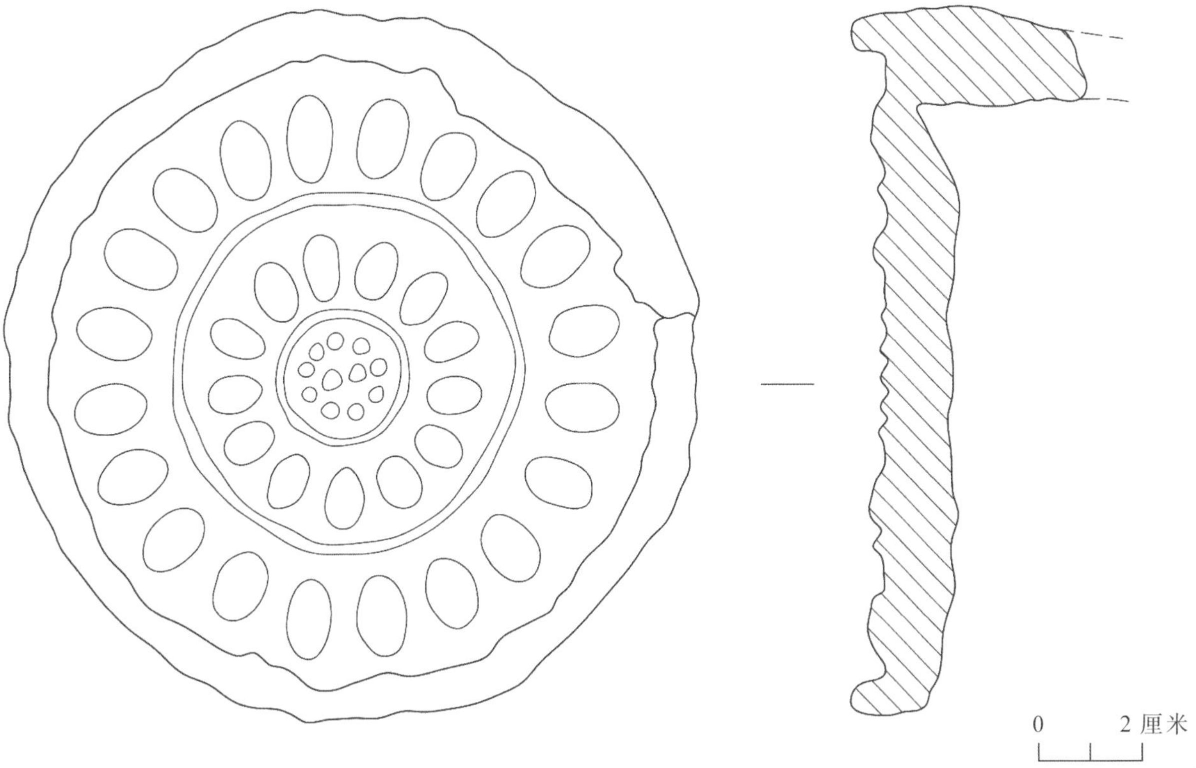

094 陶瓦当
Pottery Eaves Tile

唐

月城遗址采集

直径 13 厘米、厚 1.2 厘米

夹砂灰陶质。圆饼形，身部残缺。端面外表有一周凸棱，微残。端面外表凸印变体莲花纹。

095 青釉瓷碗
Green Glazed Porcelain Bowl

五代
月城遗址采集
口径 19.6 厘米、底径 10 厘米、高 5.5 厘米

青釉瓷质。敞口，圆唇，沿略外翻，斜弧腹，平底略内凹。口大，浅腹，内底和外底均有点状支烧痕。通体施青釉，外壁下腹及外底无釉，胎质较硬。

096　青瓷碗
Celadon Bowl

宋

月城遗址采集

口径 14.3 厘米、底径 16.7 厘米、高 6.7 厘米

青瓷质。敞口，尖圆唇，斜弧腹，圈足。唇部宽厚，足部略高，足端较宽平。通体施青釉，内底、外壁底部和足部均无釉，胎质较硬。

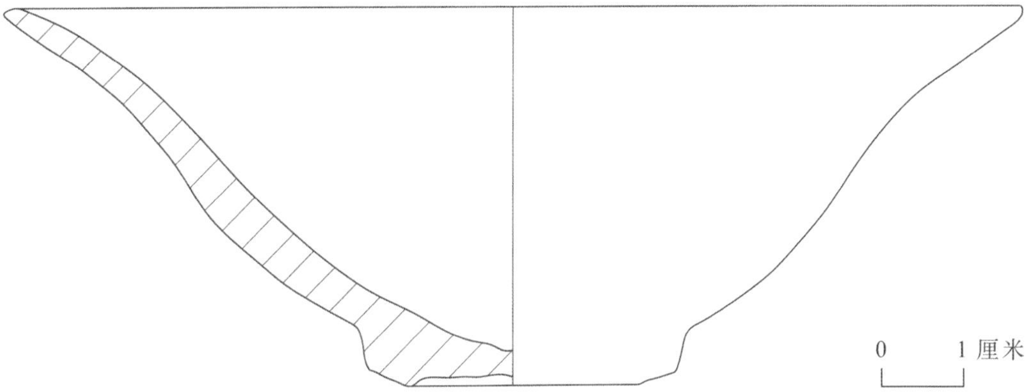

097 黑釉盏
Black Glazed Calyx

宋

月城遗址采集

口径 12.2 厘米、底径 3.8 厘米、高 4.3 厘米

釉陶质。侈口，沿外翻，尖圆唇，斜弧腹，小足略内凹。通体施黑釉，口沿处呈褐色，外底足无釉，胎质较硬。

098　青瓷盂

Celadon Bowl

宋

马鞍溪遗址采集

口径 8.6 厘米、底径 4.8 厘米、高 3.2 厘米

青瓷质。直口，尖圆唇，弧腹，平底。内外施青釉，外釉不及底，胎质较硬，夹砂。

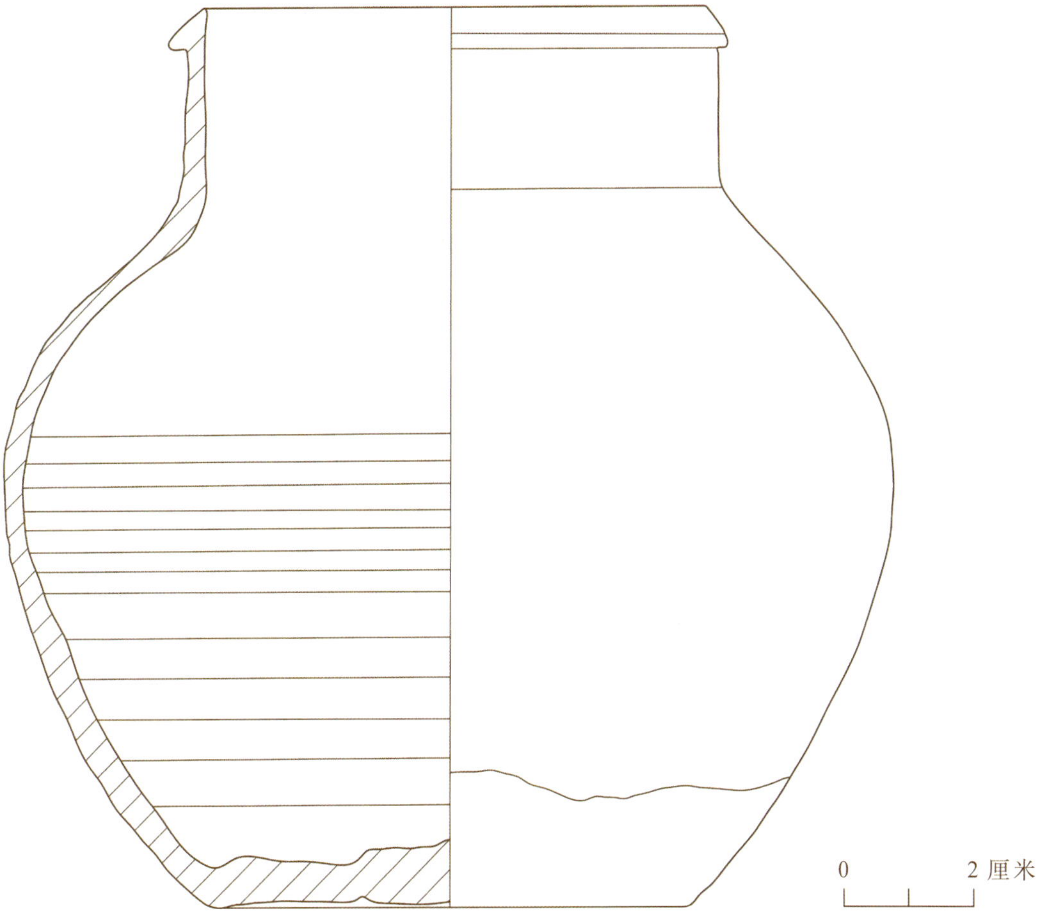

099　黑釉罐

Black Glazed Jar

宋

征集

口径 7.7 厘米、底径 8.2 厘米、高 13.4 厘米

釉陶质。侈口，尖唇，斜沿，短束颈，溜肩，鼓腹，下腹斜收，平底。通体施黑釉，下腹及底部无釉，胎质较硬。

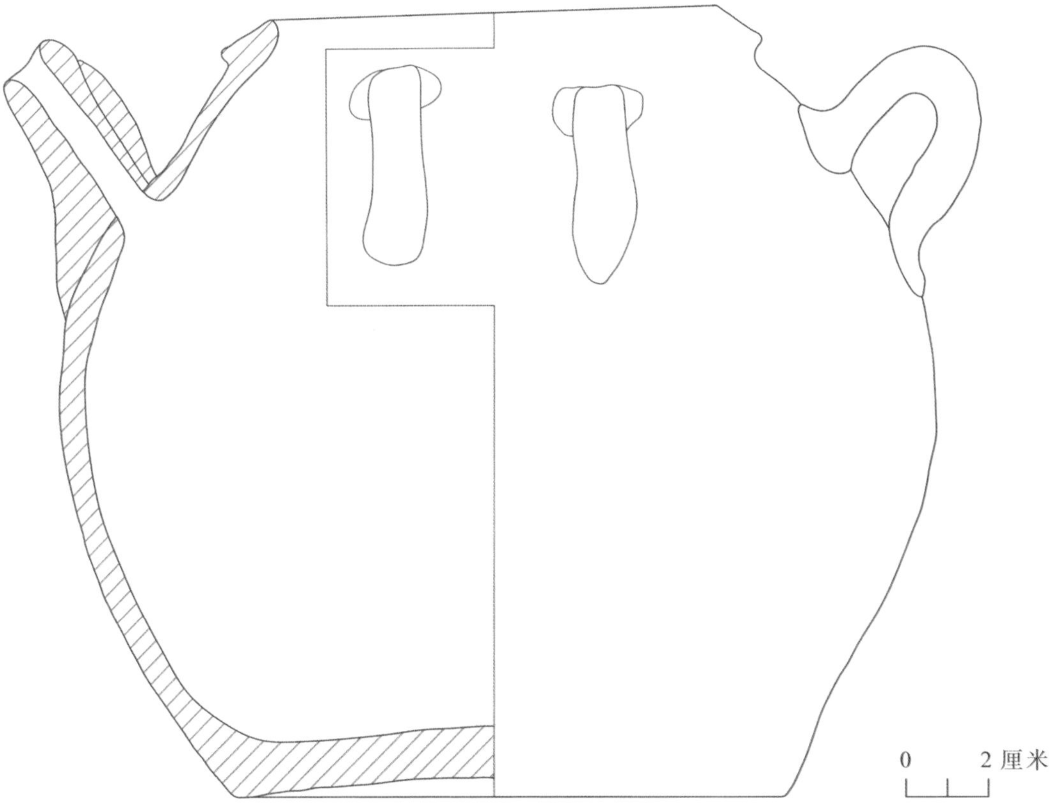

100　青釉执壶
Green Glazed Ewer

宋
月城遗址采集
口径 11 厘米、底径 12.8 厘米、高 18.2 厘米

釉陶质。直口微侈，宽斜沿，外折，溜肩，鼓腹，下腹斜收，平底略内凹。肩部斜接曲形流，对称部位贴一拱形宽执，另外两侧贴饰两对系，器身上部施酱褐釉，下腹及底部无釉，胎质较硬，夹砂。

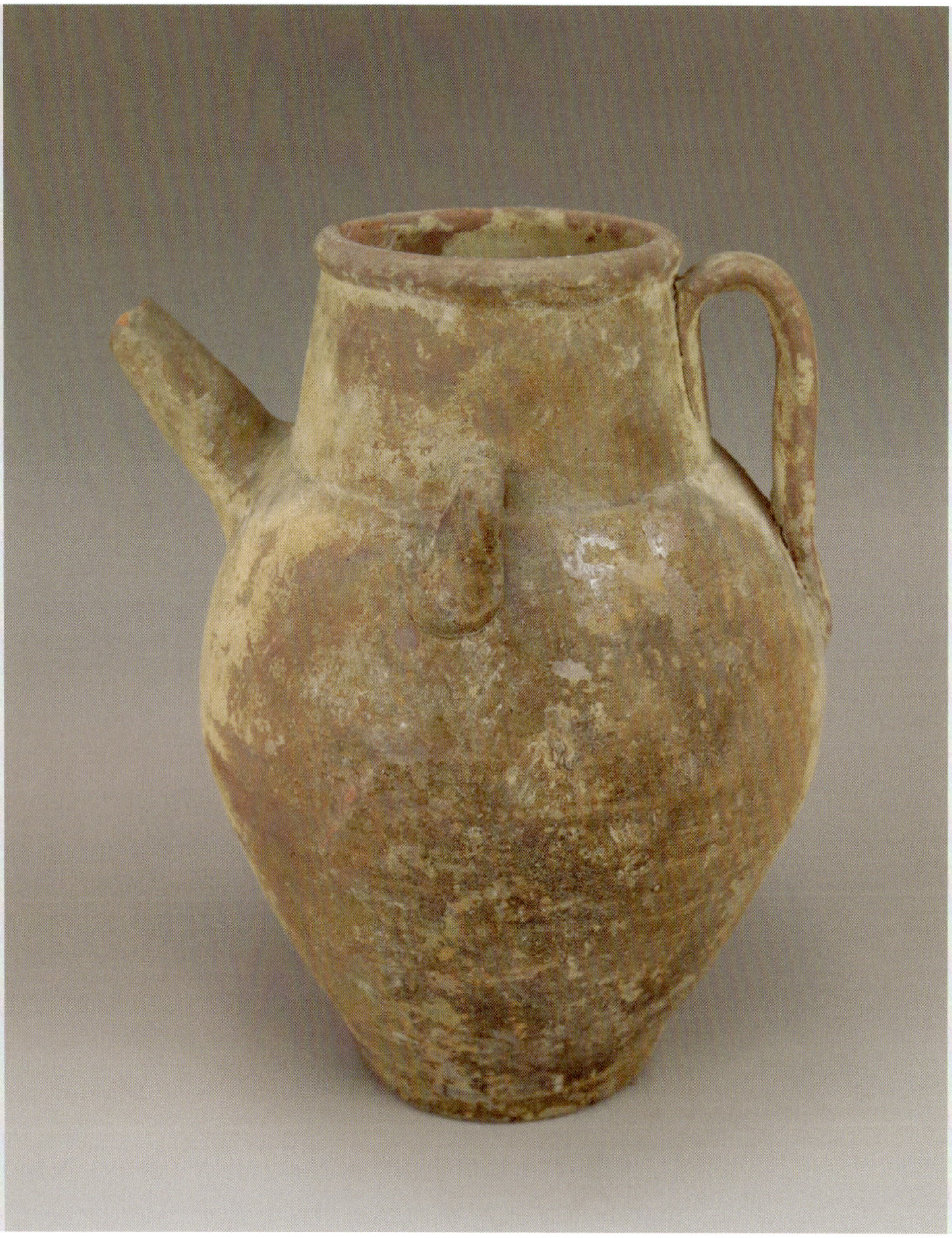

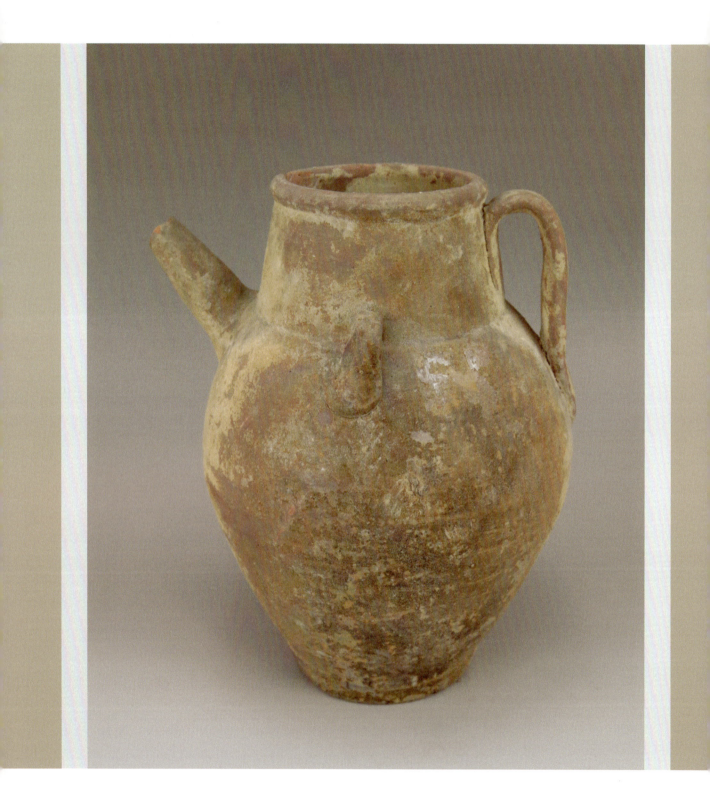

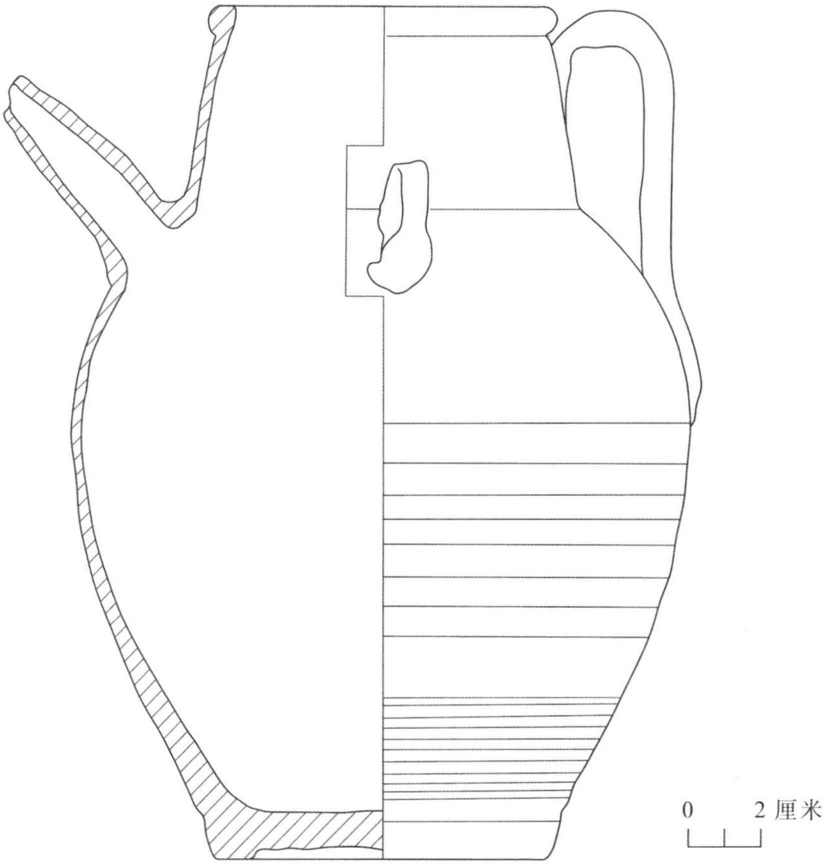

101　青釉执壶
Green Glazed Ewer

宋

月城遗址采集

口径 8.5 厘米、底径 9 厘米、高 22.8 厘米

釉陶质。直口微敛，圆唇，喇叭颈，溜肩，微鼓腹，下腹斜收，矮圈足。肩部斜接直流，对称部位贴一拱形执，另外两侧贴饰一对系，器身可见多条凹凸弦纹。通体施青釉，脱釉严重，足底无釉，胎质较硬，夹砂。

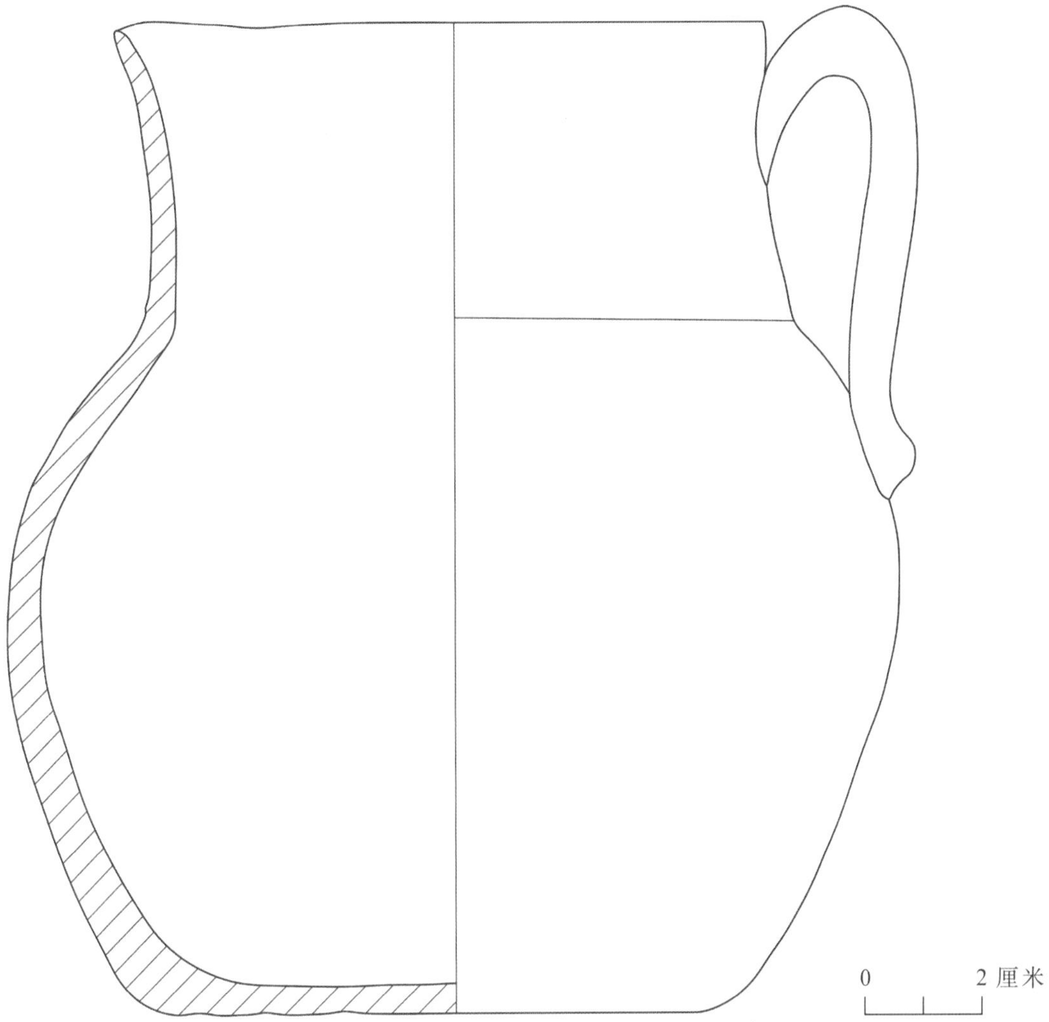

102　陶水注
Pottery Ewer

宋
月城遗址采集
最大口径 11.5 厘米、底径 10.5 厘米、高 16.7 厘米

陶质。直口，直径，鼓腹，平底。口部近似椭圆形，有凹凸流，流对面贴饰拱形执。素面，胎质较硬，夹砂。

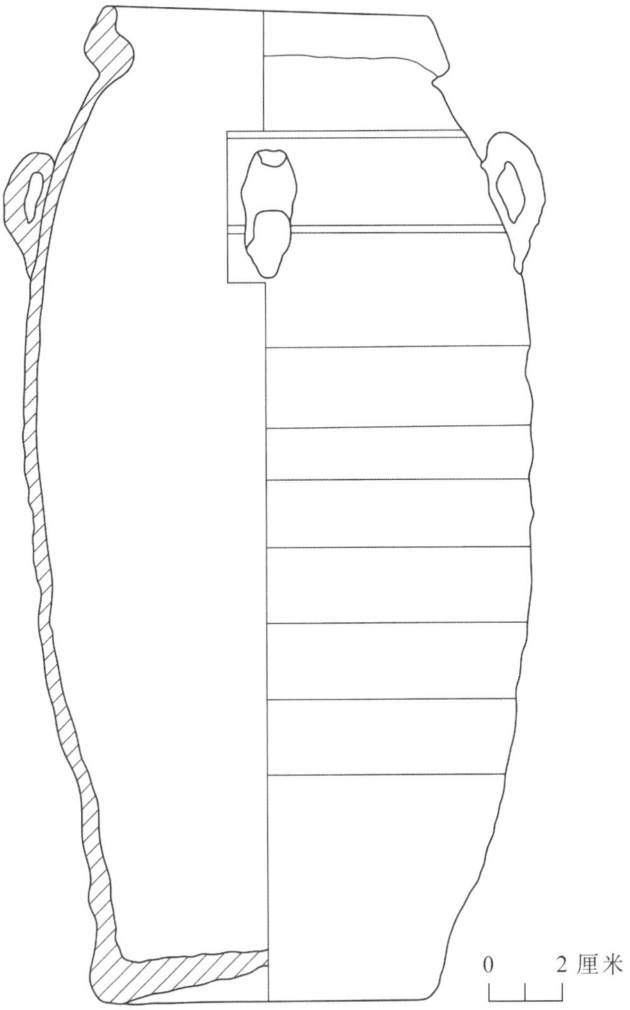

103 韩瓶
Han Vase

宋

月城遗址出土

口径 8.2 厘米、底径 9.5 厘米、高 26 厘米

夹砂硬陶质。侈口，圆厚唇，筒形腹，腹中部微鼓，小平底，内凹。近口沿处贴饰四系，器身可见多条凹凸弦纹，器身上部施青釉，下部及底部无釉。

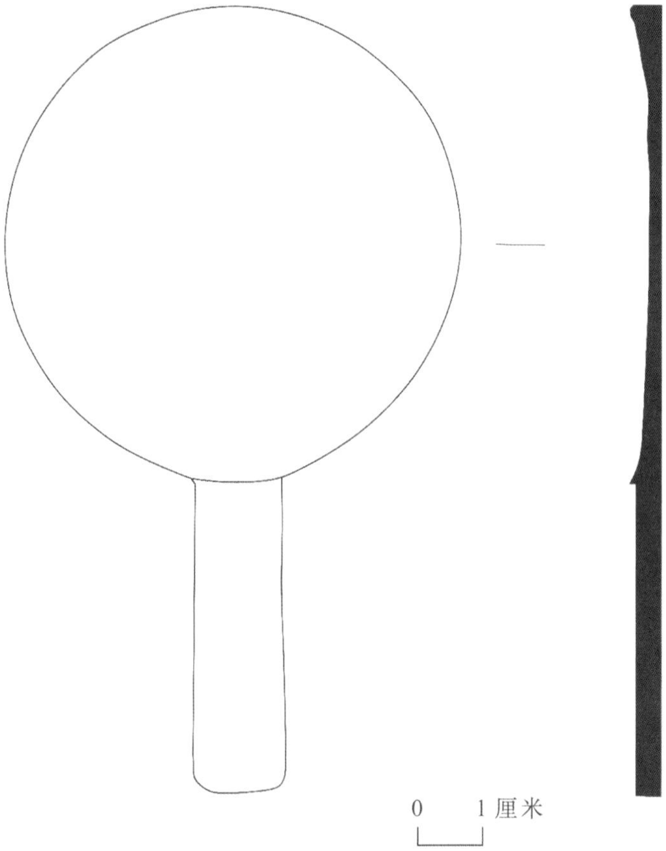

104 铜镜
Bronze Mirror

宋
螺蛳墩遗址出土（M6：1）
镜面直径7厘米、厚0.5厘米、通高11.6厘米

铜质。整体呈圆扇形。镜面圆形，正面略内凹，背面平整，长方形柄。通体光素无纹。

105　陶鸭形砚
Pottery Duck-Shaped Inkstone

宋
征集
长 15.8 厘米、宽 8.4 厘米、高 4.9 厘米

夹砂灰陶质。鸭形，游水状。鸟背及双翅为砚盖，腹部为砚池。胎质较硬。

106 铜印章
Copper Signet

元
月城遗址采集
长 2.5 厘米、宽 0.7 厘米、高 1.8 厘米

铜质。似锁形，上部为扁薄弧形穿口钮，下部为长方体状章体，阳刻八思巴字：“□ [illegible] [illegible] [illegible] [illegible]（□记印）。”

107　青白釉荷叶盖罐
Bluish White Glazed Lidded Jar

元

征集

口径 6.8 厘米、底径 6.8 厘米、通高 12 厘米

由盖和罐组成。盖呈帽形，荷叶边，蒂形钮，子口，盖身饰瓜棱纹。罐直口，圆唇，矮短颈，鼓腹，下腹斜收，隐圈足。罐身亦饰瓜棱纹。盖和罐身整体施青白釉，内壁和足底无釉。

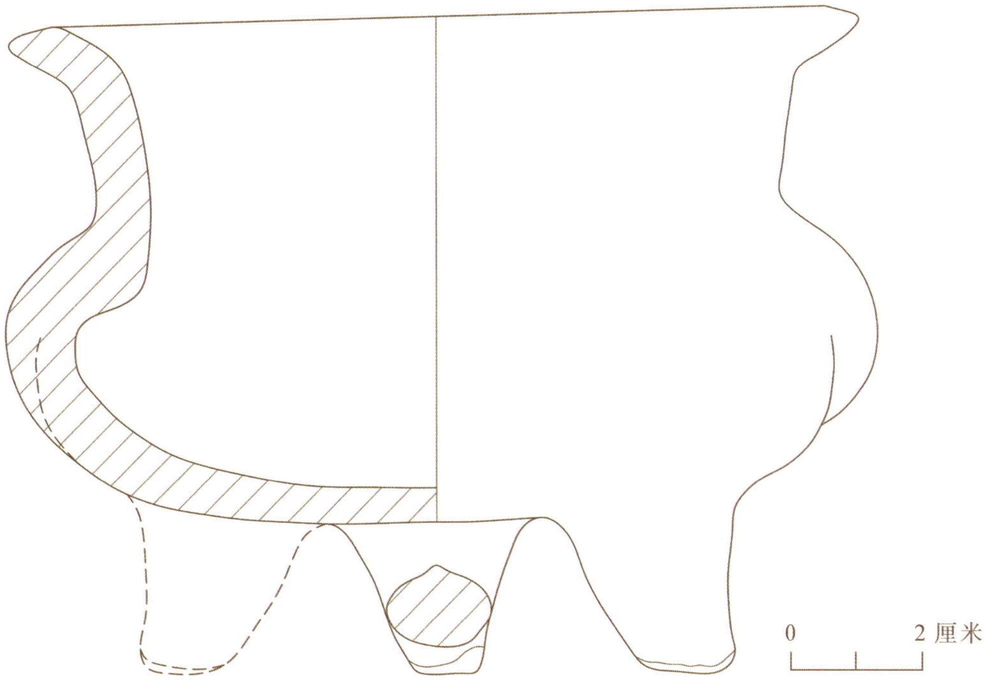

108　青瓷香炉

Celadon Incense Burner

明

征集

口径 12.4 厘米、高 10 厘米

侈口，平沿外折，尖圆唇，束颈，扁鼓腹，三圆锥足。光素无纹，足面出筋。通体施青釉，足端无釉。胎质略粗糙，釉面可见点状杂质。

0
2 厘米

109　青花瓷罐
Blue-and-White Jar

明

螺蛳墩遗址出土（M10-1：1）

口径 4.8 厘米、底径 6 厘米、高 11.1 厘米

瓷质。小直口，微侈，短颈，丰肩，鼓腹，圈足，外底微凸。外壁以弦纹间隔绘多组青花纹饰，自上而下，口沿处绘一周弦纹，颈部绘短线纹，肩部有两组双弦纹，其间另绘缠枝花卉纹，上腹部绘缠枝花卉纹，下腹绘单弦纹、双弦纹和简易仰莲纹。通体施青白釉，足端无釉。釉色略灰暗，釉下可见点状杂质。

110　青花瓷碗
Blue-and-White Bowl

明

月城遗址采集

口径 12.3 厘米、底径 5.2 厘米、高 5.7 厘米

瓷质。侈口，尖圆唇，沿外翻，斜弧腹，圈足。内底绘青花弦纹和“寿”字，外壁下部皴裂纹。通体施青白釉，外壁下部缩釉严重，足端及外底无釉。

111　青花瓷盘
Blue-and-White Dish

明
螺蛳墩遗址出土（T0503①：4）
口径 14.9 厘米、底径 8.4 厘米、高 2.7 厘米

瓷质。敞口，圆唇，斜弧腹，圈足。器身内外口沿和外底足处绘青花双弦纹，内底绘青花双弦纹和山水图。足圈较矮大，通体施青白釉，胎体较薄。

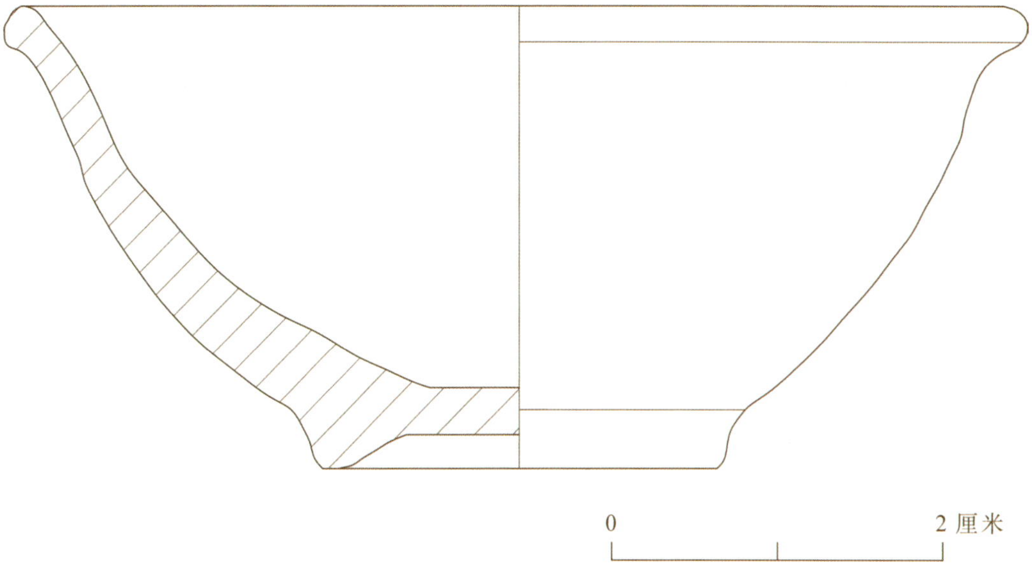

112 青瓷盏
Celadon Calyx

明

螺蛳墩遗址出土

口径 6 厘米、底径 2.3 厘米、高 2.65 厘米

青瓷质。侈口、沿微外撇，圆唇，斜弧腹，圈足。素面。通体施青釉，釉色青黄，足端及底部局部无釉。

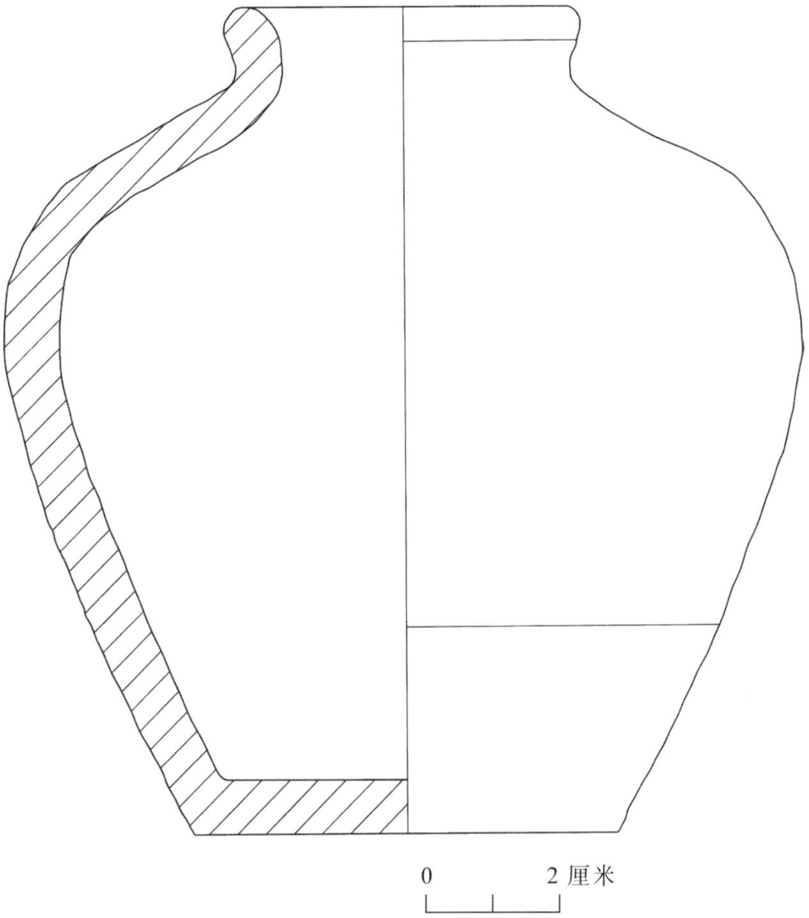

113　釉陶罐
Black Glazed Jar

明
螺蛳墩遗址出土（M10-2：2）
口径 10.3 厘米、底径 6.4 厘米、最大腹径 11.6 厘米、高 12.3 厘米

釉陶质。小口微侈，圆唇，短颈，丰肩，鼓腹，下腹斜收，小平底。器身上部均施酱黑釉，下腹及足部无釉。胎质较硬，泛红，夹砂。

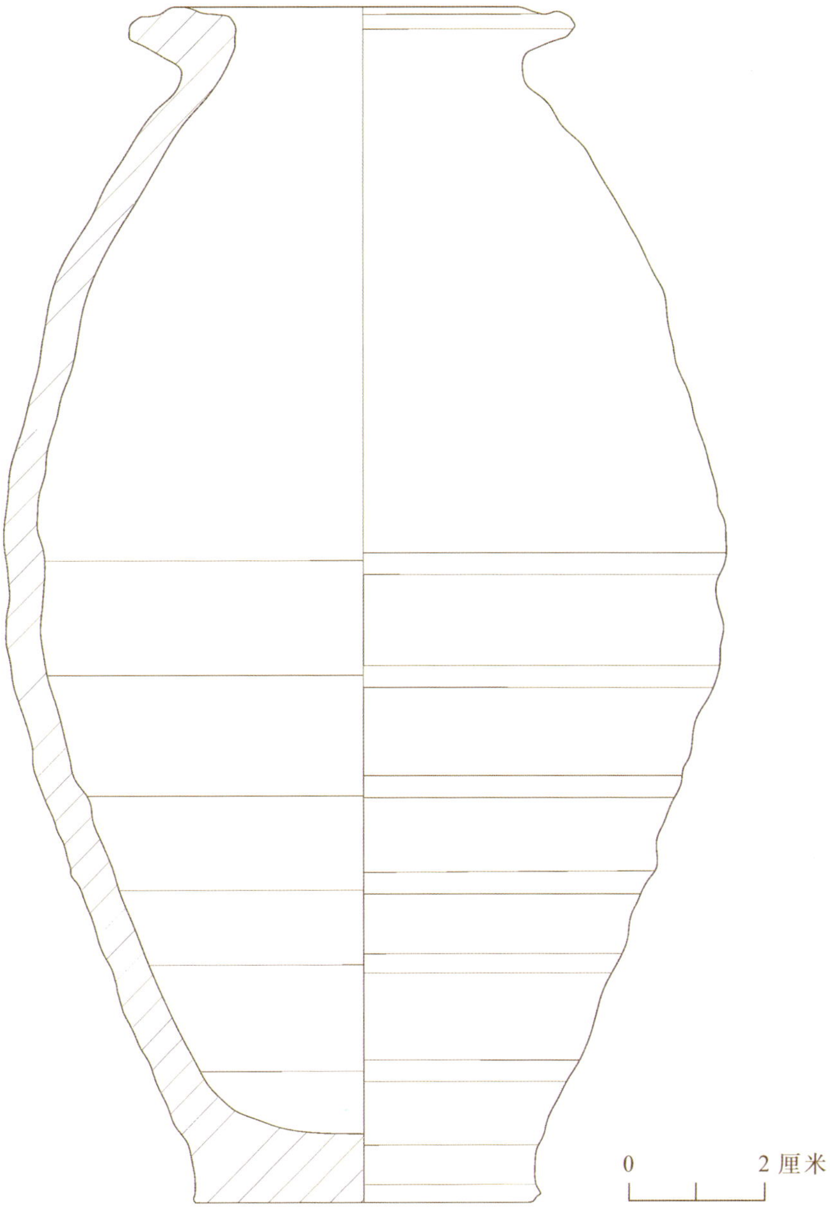

114　韩瓶

Han Vase

明

螺蛳墩遗址出土（M12-2：1）

口径 3.3 厘米、底径 4.7 厘米、高 17.2 厘米

夹砂硬陶质。小口，宽平沿，尖圆唇，束颈，溜肩，微鼓腹，小平底。无釉。

0
2厘米

115 铜镜
Bronze Mirror

明
螺蛳墩遗址出土（M13-2：1）
直径 9.9 厘米、厚 0.9 厘米

铜质。四乳四螭铜镜，圆形。正面光素，微弧起，背面中心有圆钮，带穿孔，穿孔内现存有麻绳。背面内区主体纹饰为四乳钉相间的极为简化的四螭（四虺），外区素宽。

0 1厘米

116 铜镜
Bronze Mirror

明
螺蛳墩遗址出土（M13-2：1）
直径9.6厘米、最厚0.9厘米

铜质。连弧铭文铜镜，圆形。正面光素，微弧起，背面中心有桥形钮，中空。背面内区主体纹饰自内向外由内向八连弧纹，绞丝纹和铭文带各一周组成，铭文模糊，可辨部分与“昭明镜”相似，外区光素。

0 1厘米

117　铜镜
Bronze Mirror

明

螺蛳墩遗址出土（M10-2：1）

直径 16 厘米、厚 1.5 厘米

铜质。神人龙虎画像铜镜，圆形，正面光素，微弧起，背面中心有桥形钮，中空。背面内区主体纹饰为对称布局的神人和龙虎纹，其间等距插饰四乳钉，神人端坐，龙虎腾跃，神人据考证为“东王公”和“西王母”。

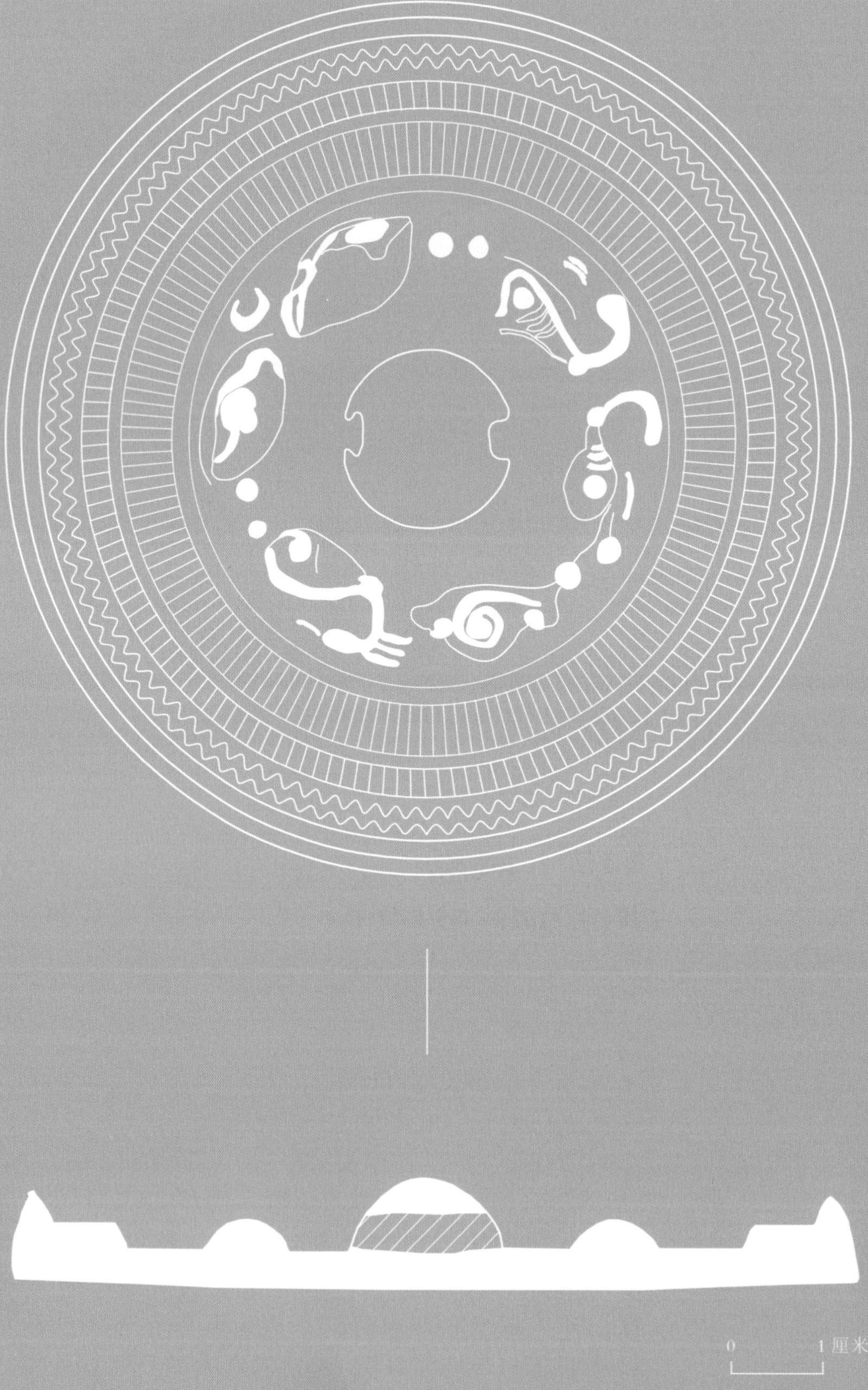
0
1 厘米

118　铜镜
Bronze Mirror

明
螺蛳墩遗址出土（M12-1：1）
直径 9.3 厘米、厚 1 厘米

三虎铜镜，圆形，正面光素，微凸，背面中心有圆钮，有穿孔，背面浮雕三虎，或首尾相逐，或两首相对。

119　铜镜
Bronze Mirror

明

征集

直径 8.1 厘米、厚 0.15 厘米、钮高 0.45 厘米

铜质。平安镜，圆形。正面平滑光素，背面亦光素无纹，中心有圆柱形穿钮，钮面有方形戳印铭文“祁□山造”。

120　铜镜
Bronze Mirror

明

征集

直径 10.4 厘米、厚 0.2 厘米、钮高 0.5 厘米

铜质。平安镜，圆形。正面平滑光素，背面亦光素无纹，中心有圆柱形穿钮，钮面有方形戳印铭文“薛思溪造”。

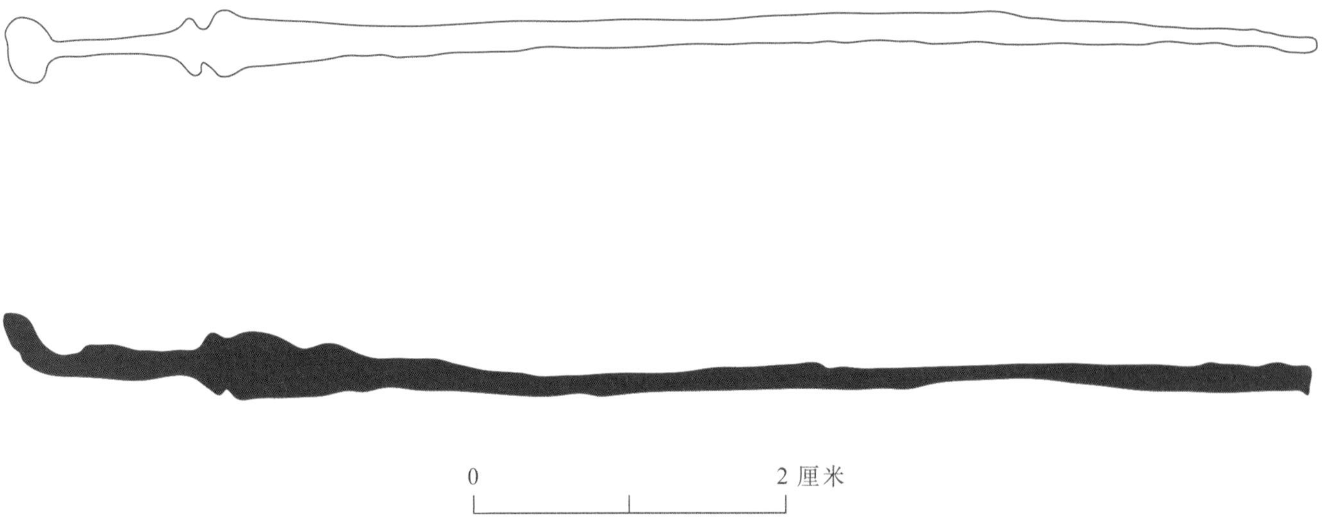

121　银耳勺
Silver Ear Pick

明

螺蛳墩遗址出土（M13-2：3）

长 8.6 厘米

银质。多棱锥形，细长，首端有凹勺，尾端尖锐。

故吳孺人楊氏墓誌銘

孺人諱妙清蘇城西南楊文政之次女母許氏也孺
人性婉順善承順與必稱所欲溫凊之禮無違
既笄適長洲吳景浩景浩嘗從外父兄仲和先生學
奇其勤敏遂以妻之佐其理家日以成事有未安者
所諫奉姑以愛敬處妯娌以和睦上下皆得其歡
心焉今而家業益昌子婦賢孝得以安享其奉豈意
中道而殁可悲也夫子男三人漢娶張氏浚娶董氏
瀾聘張氏女三人汝洎適張聰汝安適錢盛汝貞未
笄孫男三人禎祥祺孺人生于洪武己未正月二十
又七日卒于永樂甲辰九月初六日享年四十又六
卜以是年十二月十九日葬武丘鄉六都不寧之原
祔姑兆次景浩具狀請曰不幸遽失內助吾婦之賢
先生知之爲詳願徵銘堅石以垂不朽辭弗獲嗚呼
婦人之德不外稱若楊氏者烏得無聞焉諸子咸從
余問學豈可已於言乎遂按狀而銘之銘曰
務孝乎姑愛敬同相夫以正無違中以紡治家家致
隆洪德聿脩保厥躬吁壽止斯遽爾終不寧之原祔
姑封我爲銘之藏無窮

同郡顧惟寧譔并書　里士張倫篆額

122　故吴孺人杨氏墓志铭

Yang's Epitaph

明

征集

边长 46.5 厘米、厚 6.8 厘米

石质。方形，正面楷书阴刻墓志铭文，背面光素。铭文："故吴孺人杨氏墓志铭。/ 孺人讳妙清，苏城西南杨文政之次女，母许氏也。孺 / 人性婉顺，善承颜，□与必称所欲，温清之礼无违焉。/ 既笄，适长洲吴景浩。景浩尝从外父兄仲和先生学，/ 奇其勤敏，遂以妻之，佐其理家，日以成事，有未安，多 / 所谏。事奉姑以爱敬，处妯娌以和睦，上下皆得其欢 / 心焉。今而家业益昌，子妇贤孝，得以安享其奉。岂意 / 中道而殁，可悲也夫！子男三人，汉娶张氏，浚娶董氏，/ 澜聘张氏。女三人，汝洎适张聪，汝安适钱盛，汝贞未 / 笄。孙男三人，祯、祥、祺。孺人生于洪武己未（1379）正月二十 / 又七日，卒于永乐甲辰（1424）九月初六日，享年四十又六。/ 卜以是年十二月十九日葬武丘乡六都不字之原，/ 祔姑兆次。景浩具状请曰：'不幸遽失内助，吾妇之贤，/ 先生知之为详，愿徵铭坚石，以垂不朽。'辞弗获。呜呼！/ 妇人之德不外称若杨氏者，乌得无闻焉？诸子咸从 / 余问学，岂可已于言乎？遂按状而铭之。铭曰：/ '移孝于姑爱敬同，相夫以正无违中。以约治家家 / 致隆，淑德聿修保厥躬。吁寿止斯遽尔终，不字之原祔 / 姑封，我为铭之藏无穷。'/ 同郡顾惟宁撰并书。里士张伦篆额。"

賜進士[illegible]大夫[illegible]府知府邑人羅榮撰文
吳門鄉貢進士朱伸書篆
正德十五年三月甲辰致[illegible]處士吾君伯高卒孤佩瑩於故[illegible]
之北卜十有二月有[illegible]日[illegible]葬書禮也先期介里人鄒源博
吾與唐美[illegible]銘曰伯高惟一子斬焉衰絰朝夕泣拜
門謂吳墓[illegible]頌執事且又曰君諱敬高祖鄉公嘗先
事由平江[illegible]占籍溧祖景行娶吳縣陳都御史
從姑[illegible]君[illegible]二[illegible]君少有偉質稍長雖力
勤[illegible]益聞稱嗟[illegible]就外孝[illegible]定毋偕致饋義
[illegible]下御僮奴興有法術家庭外內整若畫一尤重照譜
[illegible]不苟每[illegible]子姓失學流於庸下延師家塾以便訓
[illegible]祖括至交貴皆已出一不涉昆季先
[illegible]如龍伯高者真汝曹所宜效也
[illegible]此吾家常也遂以字行耳聞心[illegible]頃刻不忘於
[illegible]視龍之為人殆無愧色可謂[illegible]守其庭訓矣
[illegible]不起越其葬之年五十有六配陸氏子男即佩
四長適[illegible]蒲次陳翔次何欽孫男二泰聘庠生莫鉉女
故兵部副郎[illegible]生孫次初安一受金鳶聘與陸[illegible]
俱吳郡子稚[illegible]情之其言動修飭知其所以狀君者皆實
錄非浮詞[illegible]其諾為之銘授其孤鐫而內諸窀穸焉銘
曰
故城之陰辛木未拱風迴水盤惟君之壟
有[illegible]履事[illegible]不朽者人匪石是憑

123　明故秋淮处士居君伯高墓志铭

Bo gao's Epitaph

明

征集

边长 50 厘米、厚 10.8 厘米

石质。方形，正面楷书阴刻墓志铭文，背面光素。铭文："明故秋淮处士居君伯高墓志铭。/ 赐进士出身、中顺大夫、福建建宁府知府、邑人罗柔撰文。/ 吴门乡贡进士朱伸书篆。/ 正德十五年（1520）三月甲辰，秋淮处士居君伯高卒，孤佩茔于故城 / 之北，卜十有二月有六日畐遂丧事礼也，先期介里人邹源慱、/ 吾甥唐美之以□丧乞铭，曰：'伯高惟一子，斩焉衰绖，朝夕苫埂 / 间，惟是墓中之石，敢以烦执事。'且又曰：'君讳敞。高祖乡公当元 / 季由平江迁无锡□□亭□占籍。至祖景行，娶吴县陈都御史 / 从姑生。父昂，娶□氏生君及二兄一弟。君少有伟质，稍长，能力 / 勤□□事□分异益开拓产业，去华就朴，孝眷父母备致，□美 / □□□□□御僮奴，具有法制，家庭外内整若画一，尤重无诰，/ 慎□□毫□不苟。每惧子姓失学流于庸下，延师家塾以便训 / 习，□□□□□□执礼，自祖括至窆，费皆己出，一不涉昆季，先 / 是众□读伏波《戒子书》，顾君曰：'如龙伯高者，真汝曹所宜效也。/ □字之君喜曰，此吾□常也。'遂以字行。耳闻心惕，顷刻不忘于 / 怀。□君考其素履，视龙之为人，殆无愧色，可谓□守其庭训矣。/ 至是遘疾□不起，数其享之年五十有六。配陆氏，子男即佩。女 / 四：长适浦熠，次潘拱，次陈翔，次何钦。孙男二，泰聘庠生莫锐□ / 故兵部副郎陈□先生孙，次幼女一，受金鸾聘与陆甫。潘、陈、何 / 俱吴郡子，雅□□慱，乞□其言动修饬知，其所以状君者，皆实 / 录，非浮词也，日□欠其语，为之铭，授其孤鑱而内诸窀穸焉。铭 / 曰：/'故城之阴，宰木未拱。风回水盘，惟君之垄。/ 有□□刻，素履聿徵。不朽者人，匪石是凭。"

0
2 厘米

124　青花瓷杯

Blue-and-White Cup

清

螺蛳墩遗址出土（T0303 ② a：6）

口径 8.7 厘米、底径 3.6 厘米、高 4.3 厘米

瓷质。侈口，圆唇，弧腹，小圈足。器身外表绘青花灵芝纹。通体施青白釉，釉色略灰暗，足端无釉。

125　青花瓷碗
Blue-and-White Bowl

清
月城遗址采集
口径 17.8 厘米、底径 7.5 厘米、高 8.1 厘米

瓷质。敞口，尖圆唇，弧腹，圈足。外壁绘青花缠枝花卉纹，外底中心有青花花押款式。

126　青花瓷盘
Blue-and-White Dish

清

征集

口径 23.1 厘米、底径 13.8 厘米、高 4 厘米

敞口，弧腹，矮圈足。内壁绘青花双弦纹一周和六朵宝相花，内底绘青花双弦纹一周和一朵宝相花，外壁上下各绘青花双弦纹一周，其间等距绘青花蝙蝠三只，外底绘写青花“大清康熙年制”。

127　青花瓷碾钵
Blue-and-White Grinding Bowl

清

征集

钵口径 12.6 厘米、底径 7.4 厘米、高 4.5 厘米

碾棒长 9.8 厘米

瓷质。钵体敞口，圆厚唇，斜弧腹，饼足。外壁绘青花缠枝花卉纹，施青白釉，内壁、内底和外底无釉。碾棒近似棒形，柄端瘦小，碾端圆大。通体施青白釉，碾端无釉。

128　青花瓷洗

Blue-and-White Washer

清

征集

口径 22.8 厘米、底径 15.9 厘米、高 8.7 厘米

瓷质。敞口，宽沿外折，方唇，深弧腹，隐圈足。器身内壁满绘青花花卉纹，外壁绘青花纹。通体施青白釉，足端无釉。

129　青花瓷笔洗
Blue-and-White Brush Washer

清
征集
口径 15 厘米、底径 14.2 厘米、最大腹径 22.8 厘米、通高 13.5 厘米

瓷质。直口，鼓腹，卧足。外壁满绘青花缠枝花卉纹。通体施青白釉，足端一圈无釉，外底满釉。

130　青花瓷笔筒
Blue-and-White Brush Pot

清

征集

口径 16.1 厘米、底径 17.2 厘米、高 16 厘米

瓷质。筒状，直口，宽沿，直腹，隐圈足。器身外表满绘青花花卉纹。通体施青白釉，足端无釉。

131　青花瓷茶叶罐
Blue-and-White Caddy

清

盖颈 5.9 厘米、罐口径 3.8 厘米、宽 11.6 厘米、厚 6.9 厘米、高 16.5 厘米

瓷质。由罐盖和罐身组成。圆盖，盖顶绘青花花卉纹。罐身小直口，短颈，方肩，扁方形壶身，平底。器身外表满绘青花回纹和花卉纹，通体施青白釉，器盖内部、器身口径部、底部无釉。

132　青花瓷将军罐
Blue-and-White General Tank

清

征集

口径11.5厘米、底径14.5厘米、最大腹径20.5厘米、通高33厘米

瓷质。由罐盖和罐身组成。盖呈半圆形，宝珠钮，斜折沿，子母口。钮及盖外壁绘青花缠枝花卉纹，沿外绘青花回纹一周。罐身直口，短颈，丰肩，弧腹，腹下部渐斜收，足底端部外撇，器底内凹。口沿处绘青花花卉纹一周，肩部绘青花回纹一周，腹部满绘青花缠枝花卉纹。通体施青白釉，盖内沿和足端一圈无釉，外底满釉。

133　青花印泥盒
Blue-and-White Inkpad Box

清

征集

盒盖口径 9.3 厘米、高 2.6 厘米，盒身口径 8.5 厘米、高 3.1 厘米

由盒盖和盒身组成。盒盖顶部近平，身部弧圆，尖圆唇，绘花卉纹加“囍”字。盒身子口，斜弧腹，平底，矮圈足，绘花卉纹。盒盖与盒身通体施青白釉，口沿处和足端无釉。

134 黄釉瓷盘
Yellow Glazed Dish

清

征集

口径 23 厘米、底径 13.5 厘米、高 3.2 厘米

瓷质。敞撇口，尖圆唇，斜弧腹，矮圈足。素面，外底绘青花方形画押。通体施米黄色釉，足端无釉，外底满釉，釉色较白。

135　铜碗
Copper Bowl

清

征集

口径 13.5 厘米、底径 6 厘米、高 7.3 厘米

黄铜质。花口，弧腹，喇叭形圈足。内壁刻“S”形水波纹，内底錾刻花卉纹，外壁通体錾刻多组鸟兽花卉纹。

136　石权
Stone Weight

明清
月城遗址采集
高 6 厘米

石质。似梨形，微残，上部尖圆有穿孔，弧腹，底部较大略平内凹。器身略粗糙。

137　石权
Stone Weight

明清
月城遗址采集
高 6.2 厘米

似梨形，上部尖圆有穿孔，弧腹，底部较大略平内凹。器身略粗糙。

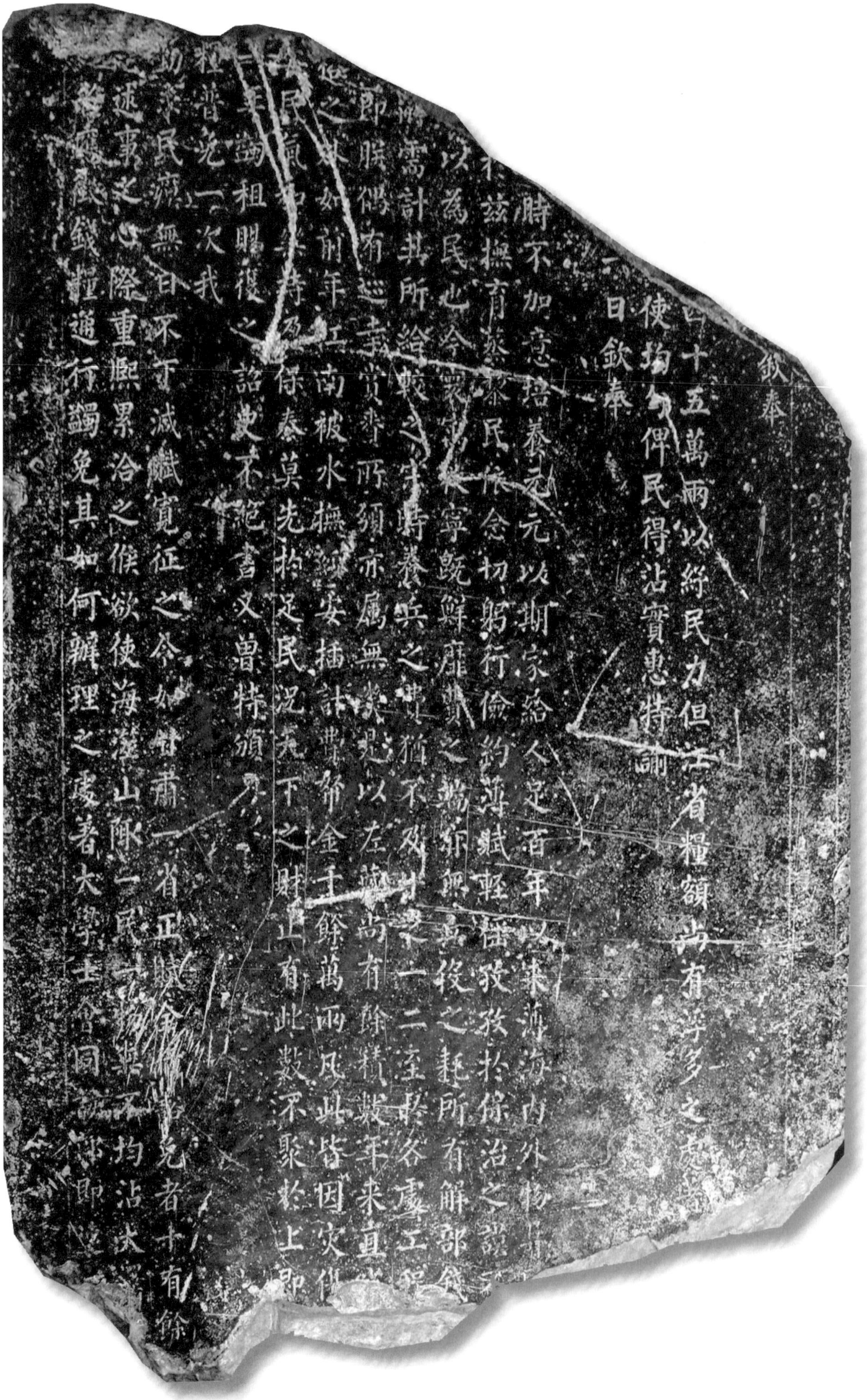
欽奉
四十五萬兩以紓民力但江省糧額尚有浮多之處
使均勻俾民得沾實惠特諭
日欽奉
時不加意培養元元以期家給人足百年以來海內外
在茲撫育蒸黎民依念切躬行儉約薄賦輕徭致於保治之
以為民也今寰宇既鮮靡費之端錙銖所有解部
需計其所給較之時養兵之費猶不及十之一二至於各處工程
節朕偶有巡幸賞賚所須亦屬無幾是以左藏尚有餘積數年來
巡之外如前年江南被水撫綏安插計費帑金千餘萬兩凡此皆因災
民氣和年特為保泰莫先於足民況天下之財止有此數不聚於上即
三年蠲租賜復之詔史不絕書又曾特頒
糧普免一次我
勤恤民瘼無日不減賦寬征之令如甘肅一省正賦全免者十有餘
之心際重熙累洽之候欲使海澨山陬一民一物無不均沾
錢糧通行蠲免其如何辦理之處著大學士會同該部即速

138　蠲免银税碑
Tax Exemption Stela

清

御亭遗址采集

残高 200 厘米、宽 100 厘米、厚 30 厘米

因碑原立于大运河西岸、望亭大桥旁的纪恩亭内，又兼碑文中有“乾隆”字样，民间以为乾隆皇帝御笔，故俗称“御碑”“皇亭碑”。青石质。楷书阴刻。原碑刻于乾隆年间，并有碑帽、碑座。1938 年（一说 1940 年）夏因被风吹倒断为三截，今仅存其一。曾被作为食品店宅基石。2019 年 3 月移至望亭运河公园。铭文残损较多，主要刻记了江南因遭受水灾而奉旨减免粮税的告示。碑中部分内容可与《苏州府志》中乾隆十年（1745）六月初九日的圣旨相印证。

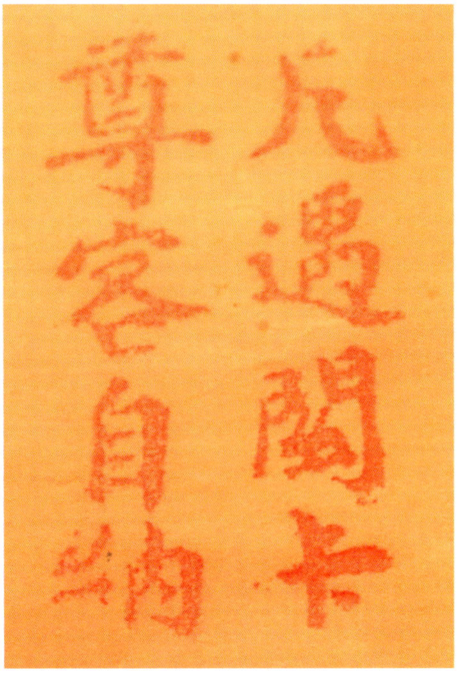

139 木印章

Woody Signet

清末民初

月城遗址采集

长 4.7 厘米、宽 2.9 厘米、高 3.1 厘米

似覆斗形长方体，上小下大，章面反向阳刻“凡遇关卡尊客自纳”。

140　浅绛彩山水棒槌瓶

Pale Crimson Mallet Bottle

民国

征集

口径 6.5 厘米、底径 6.6 厘米、高 27.7 厘米

盘口，直颈，折肩、圆筒形长腹，圈足。腹部绘浅绛彩山水人物图和题诗及款式。通体施白釉，足端无釉，外底满釉。

民國二十三年十二月
周府家宴

141　青花瓷碗
Blue-and-White Bowl

民国
征集
口径 19.6 厘米、底径 6.5 厘米、高 7.4 厘米

敞撇口，尖圆唇，斜沿外撇，浅弧腹，圈足。口沿内壁开光，绘三组花卉纹，其余满绘青花菱形方格纹，内底绘双弦纹和方格纹，口沿外壁绘折枝花卉纹，青花绘写“民国二十三年（1934）十二月”，腹部绘青花双弦纹和“介”字纹，外底青花绘写“阎府家宴”。